TALES OF THE CHINESE CULTURE

中国人的文化

上海文化出版社

Contents 目录

中国文化古老博大，对西方人来说还会觉得神秘。世界有四大文明古国，其中有三个文化发展中断，现在的文字不是当时的文字，民族也换了。只有中国，五千年来所有文化范畴的东西，都由同一个民族、同一种文字一脉相承地传下来了。中国在春秋战国时期（公元前770—前221年）就出现了一个文化高峰，后人一直无法超越它、动摇它，中国人两千多年来一直在继承发扬它，所以它是古老博大的。

2010年，上海世博会要举办了，全世界人民都想来看一看中国这块热土。这时候，如果他们看到一本小册子，能够概要性地介绍中国的文化，估计他们是不会拒绝的。有了这个想法，我开始计划写这本书了。后与上海文化出版社沟通，在双方共同策划下，最终确定了本书目录中的内容。

我一生做传媒工作，算和文化有关，我同时也是个国学爱好者，平时爱看些杂书。其实国学这个东西，主要是经、史、子、集，这是中国文化的灵魂。几千年来，经、史、子、集哺育了一代又一代社会精英——知识分子，并通过他们带动影响社会的思想意识、道德风尚和风俗习惯，使这个灵魂渗透到中国传统文化的方方面面、角角落落。所以，要介绍中国文化，如果不围绕这个灵魂，站在这个高度，就会迷失方向，舍本逐末。我在书中第一篇就提出，中国文化起源于龙文化，龙文化必会产生孔子和老子，孔子和老子思想必会产生君主制的封建社会，又由于它的过分强大的控制力，使封建社会延续了两千多年。中国周边少数民族一贯非常强大，几番统治中国，如果当时中国没有强大的文明力量来吸纳同化他们，中国的文明传承可能也早就中断了。读者看了书里面的内容，会明白这个道理。再举一个具体选材的例子：在开始写建筑篇时，因为我对建筑的知识较缺乏，就找些参考书来看，但看来看去，里面全是技术性的东西，长篇大论，像砖瓦是什么年代发明的，什么年代有了木结构构件，斗拱的样式后来有哪些变化，屋顶的形状是怎样的，等等，显然对我一点没有用处。我想了好久，认为还是应该以文化角度入手，寻找建筑的文化渊源和内涵，后来我索性全部摆脱参考材料，自己拟了提纲，写成现在这个样子，譬如，解释皇宫为什么会是这样子，四合院和文化有什么关系等。总之一句话，文字篇幅越短，越要抓住重点，不能言不及义。

另外，我在文字叙述上尽量做到深入浅出。我在自己完全掌握了内容以后，用自己的话，像讲故事一样把它们明白通畅地讲出来，还尽量穿插一些精炼的小故事，以增加可读性。

这本书用中英两种文字叙述，内容基本相同，这是为了中外兼顾。从上面介绍看，本书精炼而新颖的内容，对许多中国人来说，对他们提高文化知识也会有所帮助，尤其对中学生，它可以作为课外阅读材料。英文部分相对中文部分更简明、更通俗一些，更适合外国人看，一个外国人如果能知道这么许多中国文化，已经相当可以了。另外，中英文对照还便于学中文的外国人作为学习参考，同时也适合海外华人阅读。

周济　2009.7

Introduction

Chinese culture is old, broad and profound, and seems mysterious for foreigners as well. There are four countries boasted of their ancient civilization in the world, but, among them, three of their ancient civilization have broken up and diverted due to a variety of vicissitudes. Their present language isn't their ancient language, and their present nationality isn't their ancient nationality. Only Chinese 5,000-year-old civilization has been passed down up-to-date by the same Chinese nationality. In the Spring & Autumn Period dated back 2,500 years ago, there came forth a peak of old civilization, so lofty, so brilliant that people in later generations could never surmount or shake it, but could only inherit and expand it.

Shanghai Expo 2010 will be held soon, and by the time foreigners might be willing to pay a visit to China. During their staying, they probably won't refuse to take a book describing concisely the entire Chinese Culture.

So, I began planning to write the book.

I worked as a journalist all my life. I am also an enthusiast for Chinese ancient literature. As a matter of fact, Chinese literature was the source of Chinese culture. Ancient Chinese literature has nurtured and brought up intellectuals generation by generation, and these educated people became the pioneers bringing traditional culture into social ideology, moral code and folk custom. I realized this viewpoint must come out as the guideline of my book, as a paragraph I wrote in the initial chapter, describing: The source of Chinese culture was the dragon culture, the dragon culture must produce Confucius and Laozi, and Confucius and Laozi's doctrines must produce autocratic monarchy. More, the power of Confucius doctrine was so overwhelming that it became a contributing factor for Chinese monarchy feudalism could last a history of thousands of years. In every dynasty, the military might of ethnic minorities around the border were all powerful. They continuously invaded mainland and even several times occupied most part of Chinese territory. But after entering the mainland, it seemed, they were inevitably assimilated by and dissolved in Chinese nationality. It seemed to be a sure thing that Chinese ancient culture would also be stopped and broken up in the midway, in case of without the superiority of the lofty and brilliant old civilization.

The all essays were short, so I should pay more attention to highlight the essentials, and avoid innocuous details. I also stressed on my simple, plain and vivid style of writing in a hope making profound culture more clear and understandable.

The chapters were written both in English and Chinese. For many Chinese people, the interesting stories in the book could also improve their knowledge about their own country's cultural heritages, especially for high school students, the book could avail them as extracurricular reading materials. And for foreigners, because the English versions were more concise and popular than Chinese, the book could make easier read for them. But, the book could still help them get enough know-how about Chinese cultural traditions.

Zhou Ji   2009. 7

孔子、老子和上古思想家

中国文化的源头

　　中国数千年的传统是：政治上是皇权政体，经济上以农立国，社会意识形态是学而优则仕，以及重义轻利、乐贫安命等，这一整套文化体系，以孔子的儒家学说为核心，形成于春秋战国时期（公元前770—前221年），奠基人是孔子、老子等一批上古思想家，若再追溯上去，可以发现，它们总的来自一个源头：龙。中国传统文化是龙的文化。反过来说，龙的文化只能产生孔子、老子学说，孔子、老子学说只能产生几千年封建主义。春秋战国时期，中国由许多诸侯国分治，互相攻打吞并，各国广招人才，谋求富国强兵之道，催生了许多思想家著书立说，中国历史上出现一个光辉的学术思想活跃时期，称为"百家争鸣"。儒家在春秋时期只是百家中的一家，到汉代，即自公元前200年起，它的学说被确立为官方统治思想，进行自上而下推行。更值得注意的是，这些上古思想家创立学说，一下子达到历史顶峰，数千年来人们智慧无法超过。到了历史后期，中国由于没有新的学术思想引导，造成封建主义延续，辉煌的古老文明成了社会进步的绊脚石，这一局面直到西方民主自由思想输入以后才被打破，请参阅最后一篇《东西方文化交流》。

孔子雕像

孔子和孟子

孔子（公元前551—前479年），名丘，山东曲阜人。他创立儒家学说，政治主张的核心是推行仁政，就是要君王爱民，反对滥施刑罚。同时，他对老百姓提倡"孝、悌、忠、信"，就是，对父母要孝，对同辈要友爱，对君王要忠，对朋友要信。孔子要求读书人应有远大抱负，能"修身、齐家、治国、平天下"。孔子曾经当了三个月的鲁国宰相，据说政绩达到"路不拾遗，夜不闭户"。后来鲁国国君不用孔子，孔子便开始周游列国，希望有君王能采纳他的政治主张，但结果到处碰壁。孔子的游说活动失败，只好回家当一名教师。他有学生三千，其中贤者七十二人。孔子在教育中突出德育，要求学生在求知识以前，先提高道德修养。他还讲了许多做人的道理，如："和为贵"（提倡和睦或和谐）；"见贤思齐"（学习别人优点）；"四海之内，皆兄弟也"等等。他自己为人师表，不追名逐利，学习不厌，诲人不倦，学风也比较实在，他要求学生"知之为知之，不知为不知"，不懂不要装懂，有学生问他，死是怎么一回事，他回答是"不知生，怎知死"，他从来不说神仙鬼怪的事。

儒家的思想体系集中反映在一本叫《论语》的书里，这是孔子死后，由他的弟子追思汇集而成的。《论语》数千年来被当作入学儿童的必读教材，也是读书人的行为道德准则。

孔子死后被尊为"至圣先师"，历代皇帝给他封官越来越大，在他的家乡山东曲阜建起规模宏大的孔庙，接着在全国许多中小城市也都建立孔庙，每年举行祭祀活动。今天，孔子家乡山东曲阜成了群众旅游的热土，由孔庙、孔府和孔林三个景点组成。孔庙前面已提到，孔府是孔子的子孙居住的府第，级别仅次于皇宫。孔林里最早的林木，据说是孔子死后，他的弟子从各自家乡迁来，种在孔子的墓旁，而后发展成一片大

孔庙

树林。

　　到了战国时期，孟子（约公元前372—289年）继承和发扬孔子学说，他进一步提出"民为贵，国家次之，君为轻"的口号，在皇权体制下，他提出这样的口号确实非常难得。孟子对老百姓要求"老吾老，以及人之老，幼吾幼，以及人之幼"，意思是，尊敬自家的老人，再尊敬人家的老人，爱护自家的小孩，再爱护人家的小孩，这正是今天人们提倡的敬老爱幼思想。孟子还有一句有名的话，叫"善养浩然之气"。浩然之气就是坚持正义、无所畏惧的气概。孟子喜欢

孟子画像

找其他学派持不同观点的人辩论，他所写的《孟子》一书善于雄辩，说理生动，逻辑性强，气势磅礴，捍卫和发展了孔子学说，所以后世称孟子为"亚圣"，把他的学说和孔子的学说合称"孔孟之道"。人们认为，孔孟学说是一种"入世"，就是治理国家社会的学说。

老子和庄子

　　老子，道家的创始人，他和孔子是同时代人，姓李名耳，河南鹿邑人。道家学说被认为是"出世"，就是超脱社会的学说。老子曾经当过政府管理图书的官，后来打算归隐山林，骑了一头青牛出函谷关，被守关的官员留下，写了一本五千字的书，书名就叫《老子》，又叫《道德经》。老子的"道"的学说"恍兮惚兮"、"玄而又玄"，十分深奥难懂，他在书里一开头就说他的"道"是个说不清楚的东西，它看不见，摸不着，早于天地就存在，大到无所不包，它有个生命之门，从这里产生一种物体，一分二，二分四，分至无穷，才形成世界万物。但老子在书里讲了许多有益哲理，说"道"做事不居功，帮助万物生长而自己不当主宰。他主张做人不要锋芒毕露，要"处下"、"居后"，好胜者往往会失败，谦虚者往往会成功，主张低调做人，知足常乐，功成身退。他还提出矛盾可以转换的道理，如"以弱胜强，以柔克刚，以静制动，以退为进"和"祸兮福所倚，福兮祸所伏"等等。

老子像　　　　　　　　　　　　　　《道德经》

在政治上，老子主张"无为而治"，对社会不要去管理，他认为社会上种种问题，都是因为人们有了智慧才产生的，人聪明了，制定了法令，这才出现强盗小偷，所以他主张"绝圣弃智"、"绝仁弃义"，回归到原始社会去。他所描绘的一幅社会生活的理想图画是："国家小（部落），人口少，不用工具；虽有车船不用，虽有兵甲不用，百姓没有智慧，不动脑子，仍旧结绳记事，吃得饱饱的，穿得暖暖的，安享他们的生活，邻国就在附近，听得见那边鸡狗的叫声，但人们老死不相往来。"

庄子，名周，和孟子同时代人。他继承老子学说，著有《庄子》一书，又名《南华经》，而思想更加虚无消极。庄子说世界上好和坏、是和非、美和丑、生和死都是没有区别的，彭祖活到三百岁最短命，夭折的婴儿最长寿。又说，一个人杀人放火，一个人乐善好施，一个为利，一个为名，是没有两样的。因为从道家看来，人活着时不断追求，死后"荒冢一堆草没了"，一切不再有意义，所以庄子要人做到无是非、无成败、无梦醒，并通过修炼，达到无生死、无古今，不怕火烧、不怕水淹，到这时候也就是所谓得道成仙了。

不过《庄子》一书文字非常生动华美，视觉开阔，想象丰富，说理精辟，许多句子还有韵律，所以它的文学价值很高。历代政治家和知识分子有不少信奉道家，特别是当有些人遇到挫折，或是人到老年，他们就会从"老庄"的处世哲学里，找到自己心灵清静的天地。

其他学派和诸子

墨家学派 墨家学派的创始人是墨子，姓墨名翟。他出身下层平民，因此他的学说反映了老百姓的要求。他提出最主要的口号是"兼爱"和"非攻"。兼爱就是各阶层人们都要互相敬爱，非攻就是反对一国攻击别国。此外，他反对厚葬，就是贵族死后，不要把许多金银财宝带进墓里，要求统治者实行节约，减少开支，他的这些主张都有利于改善民生和发展经济。墨家的影响很大，当时许多人把墨家和孔子的儒家相提并论。

墨翟画像

法家学派 法家主张法治，战国初期秦国出了个法家重要的代表人物商鞅，他辅佐野心勃勃的秦孝公实行变法，革除弊政，厉行法治，使秦国很快强盛起来，后来秦始皇在这基础上打败六国，统一中国。不过秦国的法治变成了历史上骇人听闻的暴政。

兵家学派 春秋战国时期出现了大批军事家，许多人功勋卓著，名垂青史，其中最著名的要算孙武，他总结战争经验，写成《孙子兵法》一书，成为千年兵家宝典。像书中所说"知己知彼"、"虚则实之，实则虚之"、"声东击西"等，今天还成为人们日常生活用语，而且被广泛运用到商业、外交等领域。

纵横家学派 纵横家拿现在的话说，就是外交家。战国时期的纵横家专门串联一些国家，反对一些国家，其代表人物是苏秦和张仪。苏秦说服六国诸侯结成联盟，共同抗击秦国，他担任了六国宰相，后来六国联盟被张仪拆散。关于苏秦，有个"悬梁刺股"的故事：他第一次游说诸侯失败，钱用光了，回到家里衣服褴褛，面有菜色，进门时妻子不给他烧饭吃，嫂子在织布机上连头也不抬一下。他受了刺激就发愤读书，晚上拿绳子把自己的头发吊在屋梁上，旁边放一把锥子，想睡觉时就用锥子刺自己的大腿。数年后他学问大有长进，再去游说诸侯终于成了六国宰相。他衣锦还乡，嫂子很远就跪在地上，苏秦问她为什么"先倨后恭"（以前傲慢，现在卑恭）？嫂子回答说，因为你现在"位尊多金"（官位高，金钱多）。苏秦听了长叹一声，觉得一个人活在世上，官和钱"岂可忽乎哉"。

名家学派　名家主要是对事物的名和实进行辩论，学派的一个著名人物叫公孙龙，他有一句名言叫"白马非马"。白马明明是马，他硬说不是马。但他也有道理，白马指的是具体的一匹马，而单独一个马字，是马的笼统的概念，所以白马和马是偏和全的关系。

其他更多的学派就不再一一赘述了。最后重复一句，以上说的春秋战国时期各派学术思想，虽然十分简单扼要，但这是中华数千年文化和文明的思想基础。

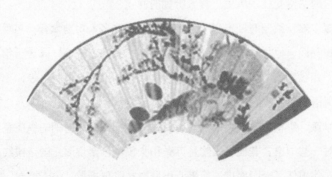

Chapter 1
Confucius, Laozi And Other Early Philosophers

Source of Chinese Culture

The main tradition of Chinese history over thousands of years featured: imperial system in politics, agricultural system in economy, and Confucius and Laozi's teachings in social ideology, that began to take shape during the Spring & Autumn and Warring States periods (770—221 BC). But the tradition could further be traced back to the earliest source: the Dragon. In other words, the dragon culture could only produce Confucius and Laozi, and the Confucius and Laozi's teachings could only produce feudalism through long history. During the Spring & Autumn and Warring States periods, there were tens of independent sub-states conquering each other, and the emperors were eager to meet some wise men and their advice — the weapon that could make their states stronger. The special time has really made many great philosophers and strategists who created their academic schools and offering their scholarly works, and was known as the unique time of "Contention of A Hundred Schools of Thought". Confucius was by then one of these scholars. The theories and doctrines created by these scholars had reached its top so high that none of any scholars in later dynasties could go beyond them. Probably, the control of Confucius' doctrine was too overwhelming in history, and there was no room left for freedom of thinking anymore, something like none of any small plants could grow up under the shadow of a big tree. As a result, China's brilliant ancient civilization had turned out to be a barrier kept China from advancing further ahead.

Confucius & Mengcius

Confucius (551—479 BC) , his family name was Kong, and given name was Qiu, a Shandong native, was the founder of Ru school. His theory about politics could summarized into two words:"benevolence" (emperors should love their people) and "etiquette" (establishing a hierarchy system and every person should stick to their own status). He also called for people to have individual morals, mostly featuring filial piety

confucius' class

(toward parents), affection (to brothers), honesty (to friends), and loyalty (to emperor), and called for intellectuals to cultivate themselves aspirant to manage country affairs. Confucius had been the premier with Lu State (in south Shandong Province) for three months and achieved big, describing "people won't take any stuff left by the roadside and doors weren't bolted at night". But he was quickly dismissed by the Lu emperor. He tried to offer his theory to other emperors, yet all of his efforts were failed, and finally he couldn't but set his career teaching students in his native state. As a teacher, he formed a norm for his students "put promoting moral integrity prior to learning knowledge". His teachings were collected and compiled by his student into a book named *Lun Yu*, literally meaning commentary words, which, through thousands of years, were the guiding code for people's ideology and behavior, as well as the textbook for school boys for their initial education.

It was in Han Dynasty (206 BC—25 AD) that the emperor honored Confucius' doctrine as the country's official ideology, and Confucius began to win the laurel as "The Teacher of Supreme Sage", and a great temple was built in his native town where the ritual ceremony was held in his memory annually. Now, Confucius Temple, along with Confucius Residence and Confucius Tomb, have become a hot resort receiving visitors both from home and abroad.

Mengcius (372—289 BC) was the successor of Confucius' doctrine in the Warring States Period. He advocated "People are superior, and emperors are inferior", an unique view commendable appearing at that time. He had also brought forward a famous word, sounded: "Respect one's own parents, and respect other's parents; love one's own kids, and love other's kids", a moral code that is promoted by the present-time government. Mengcius liked to dispute with other scholars, and in his book *Mengcius*, his viewpoints were penetrating, his logic was convincing, and his words were eloquent. So, he was honored with the title of "Second Sage". People put Confucius and Mengcius' teachings together, and gave them a combined name as "Con-Meng Doctrine". People held that Con-Meng philosophy was a kind of "inside-world philosophy", that instructed people how to act as an honest man and how to manage individual, social and state affairs.

Laozi & Zhuangzi

Laozi was the founder of Taoism School, his family name was Li, and given name was Er, a native of Henan Province. People held that Taoism doctrine was a kind of "outside-world philosophy", as it advised people to withdraw from worldly life. Laozi had been a functionary of a library, and when he was going to seclude himself by riding a buffalo, he was stopped by an official at Hangu Pass, one of the gates along the Great Wall, and was asked to write a book before his disappearance. Laozi assented and wrote down his classical book *Laozi*, also named *Taoism Bible*. Laozi's theory was too fantastic and mysterious, and therefore was hard to understand. In the beginning of the book, he declared his so-called "Tao" was a thing indescribable, neither to be seen, nor to be touched. It existed before the birth of the universe, and it had a "Gate of Life", from which something came out, one divided into two, two divided into four, …and finally produced all things of creation in the world. Laozi pointed out, the Tao, though as a creator, but it denied itself as the owner and ruler, so Laozi advocated a policy of, in his words "noninterference governing", i.e., gave up any management toward society and state. He also asserted, all kinds of evil things were derived from human's wisdom, because the wise men enacted the laws, then the crimes would come out, so he called for people to reject knowledge and abandon wisdom, and return back to the pure and honest society of pre-history era. But Laozi brought forward some clever ideas, such as:"the weak could defeat the strong" "retreat in order to advance" "arrogance causes failure, modesty makes success", so he advised people always to "keep low-profile manner", "feel content happy" and "retire after success".

Zhuangzi, his family name was Zhuang, given name was Zhou, was Laozi's successor. In his book *Zhuangzi* also named *South China Bible*, he explained his Taoist theory even much more mysterious and fantastic than that of Laozi. He said: Pengzu, a man enjoyed a long life of 3-hundred years was the most short-lived, while a die-young baby was a god of longevity. He also said: It's all of the same between a charitable man and a murderer, because in eye of Taoist, one was after fame, and the other after wealth. Life was only a short dream. Fame, honor, wealth, everything would all reduce to ashes after one's death.

But Taoism teaching had been accepted by a certain number of intellectuals including high officials in different dynasties, who, in their later years, found the world described in Taoism doctrine was an ideal and peaceful Garden of Eden.

Other Schools

Mo school: The core of its theory was "universal fraternity" and "stop mutual

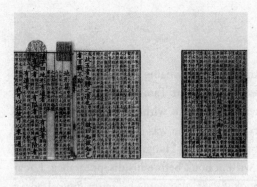

The Law of War

conquering". Its founder was Mo Di.

Legalist School: Its theory had been carried out by Qin State. Through "ruling by law", the Qin finally defeated other 6 states, and unified China.

Military School: The era saw many important military strategists, among whom, the most famous one was Sun Wu who wrote the book *The Law of War* known world-wide.

Diplomacy School: They engaged in advising some states to ally and opposing others.

There were many other schools. Though the schools mentioned and recommended above were very simple, they were really the ideological foundation of China's culture and civilization over thousands of years.

古代四大发明

中国古代文明起步早，有很多科学技术发明，例如商代的青铜器浇铸已达很高水平，春秋战国时期，打仗已有抛石机，攻城有云梯，还有能够连续放箭的连弩机（弩是强箭）。汉代早期，汉军就是用连弩来对付匈奴的骑兵。其他科技发明还包括原始的天文历法、数学以及医学等方面（中国传统医学后有详细介绍）。但其中最著名、对世界的文明进步产生巨大影响的要数指南针、火药、造纸术和印刷术，它们被称为中国古代四大发明。

指 南 针

传说黄帝和蚩尤打仗就用了指南车。黄帝和蚩尤都是五千多年前的部落领袖，由于是史前传说，这场大战也带有神话色彩。黄帝军队以虎豹狼熊为先锋，而蚩尤作起法术，用大雾把黄帝军队包围在森林里，黄帝用指南车识别方向，突出包围，冲击敌军，最后捉住蚩尤并把他杀了。黄帝教老百姓用木头造房子，用弓箭打猎，他的妻子嫘祖教老百姓种桑养蚕，缝制衣服。所以中国人把黄帝和另外一个炎帝看作是自己的祖先，称自己是炎黄子孙。

指南针的文字记载，最早出现在战国时代（公元前475—221年），名字叫"司

司南（战国时期的指南器具）

用于打仗的抛石机

南"，可能是一根小磁棒，用绳子系在中间挂起来，两头就指向南北。还有传说，秦始皇建造的阿房宫，主要的北门是用磁石砌成的，如果有刺客进来，刺客身上穿着铁甲或带着铁器，就会被吸住。有磁石，也是证明有了指南针。指南针对军队打仗十分重要，在比较长的时期里，人们一直使用"司南"这种简单的指南工具。到了宋代（公元1127—1279年）初期，人们发现了人工磁铁，就是铁在磁石上摩擦以后，同样会有磁性。这个发现对改进指南针起了很大作用，人们开始用一片很薄的带磁性的铁片，做成鱼的形状，叫指南鱼，随时可以放在水面上指方向，方便多了。后来，指南针用于航海，到宋末，航海指南针被做成了罗盘形状，就是把磁针放在一个圆盘上，圆盘画出二十四格，这样指示方向就更加清楚和精确，罗盘的名字和基本结构样式一直沿用到现在。

中国的指南针技术在公元1180年前后被传到国外，先传到阿拉伯，不久就传到欧洲。指南针为欧洲的航海家实现远洋航行以及发现新大陆，提供了极重要的条件。

火 药

火药是道士发明的，道教有炼丹术，用一只炼丹炉，里面放进无机物和有机物，加热起化学变化后，变成"仙丹"。人吃了仙丹就能延年益寿或飞天成仙（后面宗教篇要谈到道教）。道士炼丹中意外发明火药，真是种豆而得瓜。

火药发明后，很快被用于军事目的。唐代初期有一本书，最早记载了火药的配方，火药用作武器大概可分三个阶段：最初在一千多年前的宋代，有一个当兵出身的人造出了"火药火箭"，就是利用火药的爆炸力量放箭，不久，军事家又造出"霹雳炮"和"轰天雷"。北宋末,北方的金国人围攻北宋都城开封,宋军就是用轰天雷把金兵打退;第二阶段,南宋时,有人造出"突火枪",它不再是简单喷火,而是里面装了"子窝",就是原始的碎粒子弹,可以射出杀伤敌人。不久,人们又运用子弹原理,造出铜管炮和铁管炮;第三阶段,到了明代,出现更多更先进的火药武器,如,同时可以发数十支箭的"一窝蜂",同时发一百支箭的"百虎齐奔",尤其是出现了类似现代二级火箭的"火龙出水"发射器,射出的炮弹像火龙一样,先在水面上飞两三里,到接近目标时,炮弹二次爆炸,飞出火箭,燃烧敌人的船只和部队,它们能够从水面或天空远距离攻击敌人。

在宋代和元代,中国的火药也是通过阿拉伯传入欧洲。当时阿拉伯人管火药叫"中国雪",而波斯人则叫它"中国盐"。火药在欧洲资产阶级革命中,为新兴的资产阶级打败封建王朝、夺取政权起到了很大作用。

造 纸 术

中国文字起源于四千年前的商代,最早人们把字刻在乌龟壳或动物骨头上,叫甲骨文。到春秋战国,改用漆或石墨把字写在竹片或木片上。那时候,写在竹片上的一篇文章,要几个人抬,或用车拉。数百年后,又有人把字写在丝绸上,这样写字成本又太高。史料记载中国第一个造出纸的人,是东汉(公元25—220年)时的蔡伦,他是皇宫里手工作坊的一位官员,他造出的纸叫蔡侯纸,纸的原料是树皮、碎布、麻头和烂渔网等。不过,考古学家于1957年在陕西西安灞桥的一个古墓里,出土了一种纤维纸,经验证是汉武帝时代遗物,纸质虽比蔡侯纸粗糙,但时间早了两百多年,这说明中国出现纸的年代可能更早。到了南北朝,造纸技术有了改进。明末,一个名叫宋应星的人,在他所著的《天工开物》(总结古代手工技术的权威著作)一书里,详细叙述了造纸的过程:春天砍下新竹,在水里浸泡一百天,捶打去掉硬皮,再用石灰水煮八昼夜,再去除杂质,发酵,最后碾成纸浆。捞纸浆时,用特制的竹帘捞起一层薄薄的纤维,纤维堆积起来,挤去水,烘干,四边切平,纸就造好了。

公元5世纪,中国的纸已经流传到了新疆和中亚一带。唐代中期,有一次和阿拉伯人打仗,有许多唐朝士兵被俘,他们中有人会造纸,这样,造纸术就传到了阿拉伯,再由阿拉伯传到埃及,12世纪传入欧洲各国。在这以前,欧洲的贵族和教士垄断着人民受教育的权利，纸的出现，使教育逐步走向平民化了。

印 刷 术

印刷原理和印章差不多，刻印章在春秋战国年代已经很流行。汉代发明了纸以后，晋代已经有人用纸把石碑上的字复印下来，这可说是最早的印刷。也是在同时，人们开始在一块木板上刻字印刷，叫雕版印刷。1900年，在敦煌千佛洞发现一本《金

木版印刷

刚经》，印刷于868年，是迄今发现最早的印刷品，雕刻精美，染色均匀，质量已经很高，现在保存在伦敦博物馆的图书馆里。到了宋代，有一个名叫毕昇的人发明了活字印刷。因为雕版印刷的刻字很费工，用完丢弃，浪费大，活字印刷的发明在经济上和工作效率上都提高了

一大步。开始，毕昇用木头刻单个活字，但各种木头拼起来，碰到墨汁后涨性不一，造成高低不平，所以他改用黏土，把土切成一样大小，刻上字烘干，土就变得很硬。操作时，他把单个字排好版，放在松香上面，加热熔化松香，等冷却后版面就固定牢了。印刷完成后，也只要熔化松香，就可以取下活字，以备活字反复使用。到元代，有人作了改进用活木字代替黏土字，到明代，人们开始使用活铜字和活铅字，印刷质量得到进一步提高。

中国的印刷术在唐代中期传到了日本，在元代传到了波斯和埃及，然后继续传到欧洲，同时另有一路传到高加索和小亚细亚。现在，埃及已经发现了14世纪用活字印刷的《可兰经》，欧洲在15世纪也有了活字印刷。

其他科技趣闻

越王剑 1965年考古学家在湖北的望山，出土了一把青铜古剑，全国为之轰动。古剑的宝贵之处有二：一是它的铸造水平很高，二是剑柄上刻有"越王勾践自作用

剑"八个篆字。勾践的"卧薪尝胆"，几千年来被看作是民族魂的体现，因此它是一件难得的国宝。越王剑的年龄已有两千五百多岁，它全长55.6厘米，造型挺拔庄重，剑柄装饰有五彩宝石，华丽尊贵。令人惊异的是，它出土时依旧寒光四射，十分锋利，剑锋一划，二十层纸齐齐划透。剑的制造要求是，剑身要坚硬，剑刃要锋利，今天科学家在对它做化验时，发现剑身和剑刃的金属含量各不相同，这样做难度很高，专家认为是采用了两次浇铸的办法，而这种两次浇铸的技术，世界上其他先进国家是直到近代才出现的。

诸葛亮的木牛流马 三国时期的蜀国丞相诸葛亮一直被认为是智慧的化身，他制造木牛流马的故事也非常引人入胜。在行军打仗中，运送军粮是个突出困难，诸葛亮竟然画出图纸，教工匠造了上千头"木牛"和"流马"来运粮。木牛力气大，每头能载可供10人吃一个月的粮食，而流马虽然载东西少些，但可在崎岖山路间灵活行走。史书上记载有木牛流马的具体资料，如它们的形状和各个部位的尺寸，因此可以相信它们是实际存在过的。近年来，科技专家们曾经开过几次研讨会，但没有能够解开木牛流马之谜。

封建社会中后期科技停滞原因

中国是个农业文明古国，一开始土壤就不适合科技发展，占社会思想主导地位的儒家主张"学而优则仕"及"重义轻利"，这个古训数千年来一直牢牢地禁锢着人们的思想行为，各个朝代的帝王自认中国是"礼义大邦"，只重视农业，轻视并且压制商业手工业，所有学龄儿童都接受"万般皆下品，唯有读书高"的教育，千千万万人都去挤"科举考试"的独木桥，社会上都只尊重读书人，看轻所有其他行业的人，把科技说成是"雕虫小技"或"玩物丧志"，最有代表性的是唐代文学家韩愈说过一句

岳麓书院

15

"巫医乐师百工之人，君子不齿"，这是中国几千年来一直不变的大气候。其实，"利"是社会进步的推动剂，商业是发展经济的桥梁，加强商品流通才能促进工业生产发展，从而推动科技文明，但这一点在封建社会的中国不可能取得突破。近代中国也曾出现过山西和安徽商人（晋商和徽商）群体，具有相当规模和影响，但由于历史和社会的局限性，他们的目光也仅仅停留在做生意上，他们还念念不忘让子孙读书务农，在他们住宅里挂的都是"诗礼传家"及"耕读为本"一类传统的家训。

Chapter 2
Four Ancient Great Inventions

China has an early civilization, and saw many ancient scientific and technical inventions. The excellence of the bronze ware in Shang Dynasty (1562—1066 BC) and Zhou Dynasty (1100—770 BC) was the brilliant achievement of ancient melting and casting metals technology. In the Spring & Autumn and the Warring States periods (770—221 BC), there showed up a variety of weapon machines with which soldiers shot strong arrows and stones, climbed city walls, but among many inventions, what appeared most important and influential to the world culture and civilization were compass, powder, paper and printing. People usually regarded them as China's four ancient great inventions.

Compass

The word "compass" appeared at the first time in a book during the Warring States

Stamp images of four ancient great inventions

17

Period (472—221 BC) named "Pointing Southward". It was probably a small natural bar magnet, being hung up and its two ends pointing to the south and north. It had played an important role in military field. For more than one thousand years, people made use of the primitive utensil until Song Dynasty (960—1279), when someone found artificial magnet, i.e., people found a piece of iron could also be magnetized after been rubbed with a natural bar magnet. Since then, people produced a kind of small, light and fish-like compass named "Pointing Southward Fish", a great innovation that soldiers could put it on the water to affirm directions on their way moving. In late Song, the compass was further upgraded and finally transformed into a shape of plate style. Afterwards, compass has become a kind of important voyaging equipment, and made great contributions to the development of navigation industry worldwide.

China's compass spread to Arab around 1180, and soon after transferred to Europe. It served as a key technique be available for western voyagers to achieve big and discover the New Continent.

Powder

Powder was invented incidentally by a Taoist monk on his process making immortality pills in a furnace. (Taoists usually made such pills with some organic and inorganic ingredients, and they believed human beings could become immortal after taking the pills) The chemical reactions contributed to produce a new kind of material, an unexpected output, as someone describing: Sowing a bean, while harvesting a melon.

Powder was put to serve to military purpose as soon as it came into being. In early Tang Dynasty (around 700 AD) , there for the first time appeared a book recording the formula for making the powder. In Song Dynasty (around 1000) , a military expert made out a kind of "explosive arrow", soon after another expert upgraded the weapon that could shoot one hundred arrows at one shooting, called "one hundred tigers running". In Ming Dynasty (around 1400) , experts invented so-called "twice-exploded shell" which could flied toward the target and then exploded twice to assault the enemy.

In Song and Yuan dynasties, China's powder spread to Arabian and Persian areas, and then transferred to Europe. The Arabs called the powder as "Chinese snow", while Persians called the powder as "Chinese salt".

Paper

Chinese historians recorded the person who invented paper-making was Cai Lun in late Han Dynasty around 150 AD. Cai was an official in charge of imperial handicraft workshop. The raw materials of his making paper were tree skin, hemp leftover, cloth odd bits and worn-out fishing net. The technique has been gradually renovated generation by generation. In late Ming Dynasty (1369—1644) , a technician by name of Song Yingxing wrote a famous book *Wise Skills Brought out Wonders* dealt with main technical discoveries through thousands of years of Chinese history. In his book, he described in detail about the process of making paper: Cut new bamboos in early spring, soak them in the water pool for one hundred days, then hammer them into fibers and pick out harsh strings, then boiled them in lime water for eight days and nights, then ferment them, and finally make them into paper pulp.

In 5th century, Chinese paper-making skill spread to Xinjiang. Also, by the time, there broke a war between Tang and Arab troops, and Arabs captured some Chinese soldiers in battlefield who were skilled in making paper, so that the skill quickly spread to Arabian countries and Egypt. In 12th century it finally spread to Europe.

Printing

Not long after the appearance of paper, people began to print inscriptions from the stone plates in Jin Dynasty (261—420). At the same time, people also engraved words on a wood board and began to print paper works. In 1900, archaeologists found a Buddhist book from a Dunhuang ruins printed in 868 AD, the earliest printed matter been ever found and now stored up in London Museum. In Song Dynasty, a printing worker named Bi Sheng invented movable type as he realized the great waste

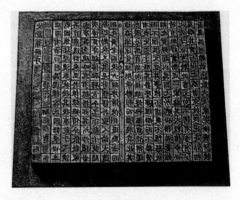

Movable type

for the once-off wood printing board. He found clay was better than wood to make type, because clay was much easier to be engraved and became solid and strong after heating. In Ming Dynasty, people used copper or tin to make type to replace clay or wood, and the quality of printing was then greatly enhanced.

Chinese printing technique spread to Japan in Tang Dynasty (618—907), and spread to Arab and Egypt in Yuan Dynasty (1260 —1368), and afterward transferred to Europe.

Stagnation of Science & Technology in Later Dynasties

As a matter of fact, the situation of Chinese feudal society didn't provide a favorable

19

soil and weather for the development of science and technology. The Confucius teachings, that monopolized social ideology called for "strive to be an official through studying hard", and all the emperors in all dynasties only put stress on developing agriculture and set restrictions to all other industries like commerce and handicrafts. A great man of letters Han Yu in Tang Dynasty has a famous and typical commentary, saying:"Educated intellectuals look down upon all men with every profession", that became an unchangeable social custom lasting for thousands of years. So, some successful businessmen in Qing Dynasty (in mid and late 19th century) , though got rich, still regarded studying (Confucius teachings) was the only broad road for their following generations, exhorting their descendants "studying" and "engaging agriculture" forever.

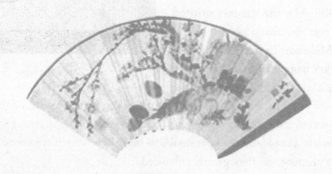

中国传统节日风俗

春 节

　　春节原来是旧历新年，新中国选用公历，然后把旧历新年改为春节，时间在公历元旦以后一个月至一个半月。春节保留了原来的传统习俗，是中国人民最重要的节日。

　　第一，全家团圆。旧历年底最后一天晚上，也就是除夕，家家户户都要全家团聚吃年夜饭，这天晚上，家长还要给孩子压岁钱。随着节日临近，过年气氛越来越浓，人心欢乐。过去都是自家杀鸡鸭、宰猪羊，还要做新衣，做糕团点心，准备其他新年用品等。过去人们还有守岁习惯，就是除夕通宵不睡觉。这些合家欢乐的习俗，现在大多数都保留了下来。

　　第二，放爆竹。爆竹的闪光和爆裂声，能制造特殊的热闹气氛。当除夕夜幕降临，就有爆竹声此起彼伏地响起，一到零点时刻，四面八方爆竹声铺天盖地，火光映天，人声鼎沸。传说中"年"是一种吃人的怪物，老百姓要用爆竹声把它吓走。原始的爆竹是用火烧竹筒，烧到竹节，就会噼啪爆裂，所以叫爆竹。

　　第三，挂春联。就是门上贴一对红

过春节（年画）

21

纸，上面写上对联，书法一般很漂亮，写的都是祈求社会和谐、生活美满和前途光明等内容。家家户户春联的鲜红颜色和吉祥语言大大增加了喜庆气氛。在三千多年前的周朝，每到新年，人们就在家门口挂两块桃木板，上面画上咒符来驱赶恶魔，所以宋代一位诗人王安石的除夕诗说："千门万户曈曈日，只把新桃换旧符。"宋代以后，人们开始用纸代替木板，今天挂春联的习俗即由此而来。

第四，走亲访友。也叫拜年，尤其是晚辈要到长辈家里祝贺新年。以前，这规矩是很大的，主人一般都要挽留客人吃点心吃饭，主人还要给来访的小孩压岁钱。

第五，民间文娱活动。春节各种文娱场所特别热闹，各种唱戏班子在戏台上轮番演出，台下人头攒动。尤其是农民自己组织起来的舞龙、舞狮、踩高跷、打莲湘等小分队，走街串巷，锣鼓喧天，到一块场地或一户人家表演，都能赚到一点赏钱。

此外，传统活动还有送灶君、贴门神、祭祖先、挂红灯笼等。

元宵节

时间在旧历元月十五日。元是第一的意思，如元旦是全年第一天，元月是全年第一月。宵指晚上，元宵就是全年第一个月圆之夜。过去中国老百姓一年到头劳动是很辛苦的，只有过年这几天是他们的假日，可以尽情玩乐，元宵节标志假日的结束，此

共赏元宵（年画）

后新一年的劳动又要开始了。

元宵节最主要的特点就是赏灯。据说西汉初（约公元前200年）皇帝挫败了一次重大宫廷政变（诸吕之乱），老百姓走上街头庆祝胜利，到晚上提着花灯载歌载舞，这天恰好是元宵节，于是元宵赏灯的传统就延续下来了。到唐代（618—907）、宋代（960—1127），民间闹元宵活动规模越来越大，场面越来越丰富多彩，除了大街小巷装饰灯牌楼、灯轮、灯树，交通路口搭台演戏外，各种化装表演队来往穿梭，锣鼓喧天，人们提着花灯上街，万人空巷，有钱人的车马一批批经过，香雾飘绕。所以，同过去相比，今天元宵灯火场面要小多了。元宵另外一个主要活动是吃汤圆，北方人就叫吃元宵，有大的小的，馅儿有甜的咸的，品种很多。汤圆的圆，也包含团圆吉祥的意思。

清 明 节

清明两个字的意思就是指天气开始清朗亮丽，万物被春风唤醒了。这个节日一般都在公历4月5日，过去有人描写"阳春三月，江南草长，杂树生花，群莺乱飞"，十六个字十分传神。人们，尤其是城里人，在蛰居一冬之后，纷纷出门，到百花盛开的景点去踏青赏花。在唐代京都长安（今陕西西安），有诗人形容清明节"待到上林花似锦，出门尽是看花人"。另外，清明节的踏青又和扫墓的习俗结合起来，以前的社会流行土葬，在这一天，人们来到亲人祖先墓前，除去四周杂草，摆几色点心瓜果，鞠躬默哀，以追念先人。今天的丧葬方式虽有改变，但清明扫墓追思先人的传统，还是流传继承下来了。

2008年开始，中国政府将清明、端午和中秋三个传统节日，规定为国家法定假日，各放假一天。

端 午 节

人们知道这是赛龙舟、吃粽子的日子，时间在农历五月初五。这个节日同样历史悠久，富有文化底蕴。战国时期，楚国在七国中疆土最大，占湖南、湖北以及整个长江三角洲地区，楚国有个大夫名屈原，有卓越才能和很大政治抱负，但楚王昏庸无能，亲小人听谗言，排斥屈原。屈原看到上下政治腐败，遍地民生凋敝，内忧外患日趋严重，而自己却不能有一点作为，感到众人像喝醉了酒，只有自己一个人醒着。于是他写了一篇长诗《离骚》，纵身跳进汨罗江自杀了。离骚意思是离别的忧伤，这篇长诗情感委婉，文字绮丽，被认为是中国诗歌史上的第一座高峰，加上他的个人崇高品格和悲剧性殉国，所以，屈原的名字千百年来受到人们景仰和歌颂。据说，当年屈原投水的那一刻，周围人们听到消息十分震惊，纷纷划着船到水上营救，因为很长时间救不到，有人就用树叶裹一点米饭，一团团丢进水里，希望鱼儿们不要去伤害屈原的身体。人们为了纪念屈原，每年到这一天都举行水上划船和向水里投饭团活动，这一传统逐渐演变成端午节赛龙舟和裹粽子的风俗。现在，全国各地端午赛龙舟活动仍然十分热闹，粽子也成为大众喜爱的时令食品，花色品种越来越多。

七 巧 节

时间在农历七月初七。初秋金风玉露开始送爽，夜空也特别皎洁透明，满天星斗，还横着一条乳白色银河。这样的美景，怪不得伴有一个美丽故事：天上玉帝有个女儿，每天织布，不注意打扮，看起来不漂亮了，玉帝就把她嫁给一个牛郎。但织女在嫁给牛郎以后，却荒废了织布，于是玉帝又开始发脾气，将夫妻俩拆开，每年只允许他们在七月七日晚上相会一次。人们看到天上有牛郎星和织女星，相隔在银河两边，每到七夕，它们的距离真的靠近了。传说这时候有成千上万只喜鹊飞到银河上，搭起一座桥，叫鹊桥。两个情人黄昏时走到鹊桥上相会，到天亮时又恋恋不舍地分手。汉代的古诗十九首中有咏牛郎织女说：迢迢牵牛星，皎皎河汉女……河汉清且浅，相去复几许？盈盈一水间，脉脉不得语。这里表达的是爱情受折磨的痛苦。但宋代词人秦观有一首七夕词说："金风玉露一相逢，便胜却人间无数……两情若是久长时，又岂在朝朝暮暮。"说的是另一种理解和韵味。

另外，古时候妇女在这个晚上还举行"向织女讨七巧"活动，大家绣花，看谁绣得快、绣得好。据说这样的活动能使妇女们心更灵、手更巧。近年来，有人提了一个有意义的建议，就是把七月七日这一天，定为中国的情人节，这个动议的结果似乎还悬而未决。

中 秋 节

中秋节时间是农历八月十五日，是列在春节后的第二个重要节日。月亮一年要圆十二回，而八月的月亮最圆、最亮，所谓"十二度月皆好看，其中圆极是中秋"。人们赏月活动的历史已很悠久，有记载唐玄宗和杨贵妃，每到中秋夜都要到太液池边望月。如遇到丰收年，节日里更是"灯火家家市，笙歌处处楼"。北宋初，皇帝正式把八月十五日这一天定为"秋节"，年年到了这个晚上，天上月圆，人间家庭团圆。到了明代、清代，人们赏月的热情有增无减。《红楼梦》里有两句诗描写中秋盛况："天上一轮才捧出，人间万姓仰头看。"非常有气派。

在中秋节，人们一边赏月，一边吃月饼，吃月饼的历史也很久了。一种说法是：唐代初的一个中秋夜，皇帝拿着一个吐蕃（藏族人）进贡的制作精美的月饼给臣子们看，然后切成小块和大家分享。另外一个流传更广的说法是：元代蒙古族残酷压迫汉人，每个村子都有一个蒙古人统治着汉族老百姓，中秋节将到，汉族老百姓在月饼里面夹一张小纸条，写着"八月十五杀鞑子"（对蒙古人的不友好称呼），互相秘密传递。可见吃月饼的风俗，在元代以前已经十分流行了。

传说月亮里边有座广寒宫，住着一个美丽仙女嫦娥，嫦娥的名字在民间家喻户晓，所以中国登月卫星也命名为嫦娥号。嫦娥是史前社会里一个部族首领的女儿，嫁给另外一个部族的勇士后羿为妻。中国神话中还有一个著名的后羿射日的故事，说是当时在天空中一共有十个太阳，全天只有白天，没有夜晚，全年没有春夏秋冬。十个太阳发威，草木枯死，山川平原都被烤成一片焦土。后羿看到百姓受十个太阳的苦，就挽起弓，搭上箭，向天瞄准，一箭射下一个太阳，连发九箭，射下九个太阳，最后留下一个，就成了现在的样子。传说中还说到，后羿还在西王母处得到一种不死药，放在家里。有一天，嫦娥趁后羿不在，出于好奇，把不死药偷吃了，后羿回家时，只见嫦娥在院子里腾空飞起，一直飞进了月宫里，从此两人人仙异途。

月亮融入了人们的生活，历代诗人写了大量的关于月亮的诗歌，所以月亮也是中国文化中不可缺少的一部分。关于中秋明月的诗歌，现在人们用来交流感情和祝愿，说得最多的是苏轼的"人有悲欢离合，月有阴晴圆缺，此事古难全。但愿人长久，千里共婵娟"。

重 阳 节

重阳节时间在农历九月九日，按传统的阴阳学说，九是阳数，双重阳数就是重阳，也叫重九。九又是十进位里最高的数字，所以还含有吉祥长寿的意思。中国人向来有重阳登高的习俗，因为那时节正是秋高气爽，风景宜人，到野外爬爬山，活动活动身躯，有利身心健康。说起登高习俗还有一个传说：东汉时候，有一个有名的术士，也就是道士，名叫费长房，他捉鬼的本领很大，九月初有一天，他看着他的一个弟子桓景的脸，说："九月九日你家有大难，你赶紧回去，九日一早，带你全家人离开家，爬到一座山顶上，每个人头上插一根茱萸条，再喝点菊花酒，可以避去灾难。"桓景听了心里十分敬畏，就按照师父指点，当天带了家人登高。到了黄昏，等到他们回到家里，发现所有家畜家禽都死光了。这个传说中有一点合理的成分是，茱萸是一种中药，它可以滋补身体里各种内脏。菊花不但供人们欣赏，泡成菊花酒，老人喝了还可以气血流通，步履轻盈。

近年来，国家把重阳节正式命名为老人节，这一方面有九九敬老的意思，另外，鼓励老人们在这个季节多到户外活动，可以增进健康，延年益寿。

Chapter 3

Folk Festivals Customs

Spring Festival

Spring Festival is the original New Year Festival in lunar calendar. After the founding of the New Republic in 1949, the government officially adopted universal calendar, and renamed the Lunar New Year as Spring Festival. The festival is still weighting heavily on people's minds, and its traditions are mostly inherited by people up-to-date. Firstly, people give the family reunion the special attention, and all the separated family members would back home. People buy new clothes, gifts, a lot of food and delis, and prepare a sumptuous "New Year Eve reunion feast". Secondly, people decorate their houses, by hanging up the red-paper couplets, paper-cuts and New Year folk paintings on their doors, windows and walls. The red and colorful decorations constitute a thick festive atmosphere everywhere. In the evening, people begin to set off firecrackers. It is said, the Chinese word "nian", literally meaning "year", was a kind of ancient killer ghost, which would be frightened by the explosions of firecrackers and running away. Usually the intensive and explosive sound of firecrackers could create the utmost glowing atmosphere of festival. Thirdly, people pay mutual visit to offer best wishes and say good luck of the coming New Year, especially, the young generation would go to elderly family to send respects to them.

Gods of Spring Festival

Lantern Festival

The festival falls on the date of Jan 15 in lunar calendar, and it is the indication of the end of the Spring Festival. The most important custom of the Lantern Festival is people appreciating a variety of lanterns after dusk setting in. It is said, in early Han Dynasty (around 200 BC) , the emperor defeated a serious coup, and the joyful people took to the streets to celebrate with lanterns in their hands. The same activity took place annually and became a habitual custom. In Tang (618—907) and Song (960—1279) dynasties, the activities of the festival reached its climax: People decorated all the streets and lanes with colorful balls, high lantern wheels, lantern trees, and a variety folk art performances showed up, such as dragon-dancing, lion-dancing, walking on stilts and beating waist-drums. Also from Song Dynasty, people began to eat sweet dumplings named "yuan", the word means good luck and family reunion. The tradition of eating "yuan" has passed down and be prevailing in present days.

Qingming Festival

The Chinese words "qing" and "ming" literally mean "clear" and "bright", and the festival falls on the days of early April, when trees and grasses begin to shoot their leafs, and hundred kinds of flowers begin to blossom. City residents, after shut themselves up all the winter days, would go for an outing to appreciate the natural beauty. The custom is called as "Stepping green". The Festival is also the day for people to pay visit to their ancestors' tombs, cherishing memories to their passed-away dear ones.

Duanwu Festival

The festival is popularly known as the day of dragon-boat competing and eating zongzi, a kind of small meat-rice pack wrapped with bamboo leafs, and it falls on the date of lunar May 5. The two customs are both in memory of a great patriotic poet Qü Yuan in the Warring States Period (475—221 BC) . Qü was a capable premier of Chu State, a state situated in the mid and lower reaches of Yangtze River, but he was dismissed by the oafish Chu emperor who believed a slander framed up on him. Being felt nothing able to do for his crisis-riddled state and disaster-suffering people, Qü composed a long poem *Woe on Departure*, a spectacular brilliant literary work, then jumped into a river and drowned himself. On hearing the sad news, people rushed out of their homes, rowing their boats searching around for him. People also made small rice packs throwing them into the water in a hope that fish should not hurt Qü's body.

People held the same activity on Qü's death anniversary, and finally the activity became the popular folk traditions.

People make Zongzi

Seven-Clever Festival

The date falls on lunar July 7, so it's also called Double Seven Day. By the time, the early autumn cool wind begins to drive out the summer's burning heat, and the starry sky lying with the Milky Way (the Silver River in Chinese) , looks clear and crystal at night, hence there was a folklore telling about "A Cowboy and a Weaving Girl" story: The Heaven Emperor had a daughter who buried herself in weaving all day and night, and the father married her off to a cowboy. But the girl, after got married, began to neglect her work that enraged her father. The Emperor then punished the girl by separating the couple, and allowed them only to meet once a year. Afterward, people could see two stars, Cowboy Star and Weaving Girl Star, separating at two opposite sides of the Silver River. It is said, in the evening of Double Seven, thousands of thousands of magpies would come up and create a magpie bridge, providing a meeting place for the poor cowboy and weaving girl, and after a short reunion, the couple would tear their goodbye at the dawn breaking.

In old time, there prevailed a custom "Learning skill from the Weaving Girl" among mass women. They competed their embroidery or other craft skills, believing that the Weaving Girl could help improve their cleverness and skillfulness. Nowadays, someone suggested the government could officially name the day as Chinese Valentine's Day.

Mid-Autumn Festival

The day falls on lunar 15th August and it is the second important festival for Chinese people. The moon turns out to be the biggest and brightest in August comparing to all other months. The custom of appreciating moon activity on Mid-August Festival boasts to have a long tradition, especially in bumper years, as been described:"Every house's floodlit, every family fills with happy music", "The round moon hangs over the sky, the round (reuniting) families celebrate on the earth". There were two poem lines in the novel *Dream of Red Mansion*:"As soon as moon rising, thousands of people crane necks watching".

At the same time watching the moon, people also eat the moon cake. It is said, during Yuan Dynasty (1260—1368) , the cruel Mongolian ruler sent every township a Mongolian soldier to supervise Han people. One year, some Han people put a piece of paper inside the moon cake, writing:"Kill the Mongolian barbarian in mid autumn evening" as a secret notice of uprising. The story convinced that the custom of eating moon cake was already popular before Yuan ruling.

There was also a legend "Chang'e Running toward Moon". The girl Chang'e was a household name among Chinese people, therefore China's moon-probing satellite is after her name. She was a daughter of the head of a pre-historical commune, and her husband Hou Yi was a brave warrior, who had a kind of immortality pills got from the Celestial Heaven Mother. One day, out of curiosity, Chang'e took stealthily a pill and ate it. When Hou Yi returned home, he saw his wife elevate from the ground and fly slowly and directly into the moon, and the couple since then had to keep separated from each other.

In Chinese history, there were many poets composing a lot of excellent poem lines to praise the moon, and the moon has become a part of Chinese culture. Among the lines, the most popular and widely-read were Su Shi's (in Song Dynasty) works: Wish my dear ones live longer years; Share with me the same moon away thousand miles.

Double-Nine Festival

Chinese people call the date of lunar September 9 as the Double-Nine Festival, or Double Yang festival. (According Chinese ancient philosophical system of Yin and Yang, the number 9 belongs to Yang number) For thousands of years, people had a custom of "ascending mountains on the Double-Nine Festival", and the custom came from an ancient legend in late Han Dynasty (AD25—220).There was a famous Taoist by name of Fei Changfang, who had supernatural power to drive away or catch ghosts. One Double 9 Eve, he said to one of his disciples named Huan Jing with a serious and urgent manner:"A calamity would set in your family on September 9, go back to your home, and take your family members to leave your house that day, and climb up a mountain. Each of you must wear a twig of cornel on your head, and then the calamity could be avoided."Huan Jing and his family did in accordance with the master's instruction. When they returned home in the evening, to their great shock and astonishment, they found out that all of their livestock in the house were dead.

In recent years, Chinese government declared the festival to be the Senior People Day, because the double 9 represents the auspicious number of longevity, and it is also good for old people to hold activities to ascend mountains or high places on fine autumn days.

汉族起源

中国人种据说是从非洲迁移过来的，但这只是科学家的推想。在中国这块土地上，考古发现最古老的人种是云南的元谋人，距今已有170万年，他们是开始直立行走的类人猿。经过漫长的石器时代，到距今7000至4000年的母系社会向父系社会转变时期，考古发现原始人遗址遍布各地。对中国原始社会的发展，历史学家认同三皇五帝的说法，但具体是哪几个三皇五帝，意见又不一致，其实三皇五帝都是原始部落的领袖，其中最著名的，一个是炎帝，又称神农氏，生活在河南省黄河流域一带；一个是黄帝，生活在陕西黄土高原及山西一带；还有一个蚩尤，生活在山东一带。后来黄帝和蚩尤两个大部落之间爆发战争，黄帝获胜，黄帝部落又和炎帝部落合并，这样，统一的华夏民族就开始形成了。后来中国人称自己为炎黄子孙，当今在河南有神农山和神农庙，在陕西有黄帝陵。现在每年都有来自世界各国的华人到黄帝陵举行祭祀活动。

那么，中华民族为什么又叫汉族呢？原来汉代（公元前206—公元220年）是中国历史上第一个强大的封建帝国，周边的少数民族人把内地人叫汉人，后来朝代变了，汉人的叫法延续下来，中国人也自称

黄帝画像

为汉人，把其他少数民族人统统叫胡人，以示区别，这里胡人的"胡"字并不含贬义。

北京猿人头盖骨

1929年考古学家在北京郊区周口店挖掘到一片猿人头盖骨化石，1937年，又出土了5个完整的猿人头盖骨和许多肢体骨骸化石。这是世界近代史上一个重大考古发现，猿人头盖骨化石距今70万年，人们称之为北京猿人。北京猿人的出现为达尔文的进化论提供了有力证据。1937年"七七"事变，日本发动侵华战争，周口店发掘工作被迫停止，猿人头盖骨化石被安放在北京协和医院里。1941年，国际局势继续恶化，为了防止化石落入日本人手里，中国政府决定把它运到美国保存。猿人头骨由一个保管员装箱，由美国海军陆战队员护送到秦皇岛，装上一艘美国邮轮，但这时候太平洋战争爆发，日本人劫持了装有猿人头骨的箱子，据说，当他们打开箱子，发现里面是空的，这个世界级珍宝从此消失，至今杳无音信。关于猿人头骨的下落，专家们众说纷纭，有人说是给日本人拿走了，有人说那艘邮轮实际上到了美国，还有人说那个保管员装箱的时候偷天换日，把真正的猿人头骨藏起来了。

少数民族的入侵和融合

在全世界，中国的地理和文化条件很独特，汉族居住在中间的地带，很早就有了高度的农业文明，周边是少数民族聚居区，统称为东夷、南蛮、西戎、北狄。北方的少数民族地区基本上以长城为界，生产和气候条件恶劣，人们逐水草而生，他们虽然经济落后，但地域广大，民族彪悍，军力强盛，不断向汉人地区进犯（在汉代、唐代强盛时，也向边境扩展疆土），因此，历代民族矛盾一直是国家存亡的关键，战争频繁。但另一方面，由于汉人的政治文化远远优于少数民族，在文化上占据强势地位，而处文化弱势的往往被淘汰和同化，所以数千年来，汉人有强大的吸纳力和同化力，少数民族在不断进犯中又不断融合进汉族中来。

中国第一次民族大融合是在魏晋南北朝时期，到南北朝，当时北方最强大的5个少数民族匈奴、鲜卑、羯、氐、羌，占领了长江以北的广大地区，建立了16个大大小小的国家，而一直统治全国的汉族政权却退缩到了长江以南。从东晋开始到南北朝，这样的南北分治局面延续了两百多年（318—581年）。中国有个传统的观念，占领了北方，主要指河南、山西、河北、山东一带，就算占领了全国。那时候长江以南还算蛮荒地区，按照这个传统，当时少数民族领袖认为，自己已经是全中国的统治者，长江以南的汉人政权只是一个不合法的小朝廷。不过，代表当时文化发展潮流的是在南方，特别是南北朝时期诗歌文赋方面取得光辉成就，南方出现了大批优秀文人。在北方，有趣的事情也发生了，这些少数民族统治者有一个共同特点，就是在建国后都声称，自己是古代汉族三皇五帝中某一个帝王的后裔；还有，他们一般都认真学习研究孔孟和别的经典，有的已经有高深的汉文化知识，所以

唐代胡人骑驼俑

纷纷仿效汉族的政治制度，推行汉化运动，最有代表性的是北魏的孝文帝，他是鲜卑族。他做皇帝后做的第一件事就是迁国都到洛阳，接着下令把鲜卑族人的姓名改为汉人的，他带头把自己原来的鲜卑人的姓拓跋，改为汉人的姓元，把原来名字也改了，他还下令要鲜卑人和汉人通婚，自己带头娶了五个汉族姑娘，叫自己六个弟弟也娶了汉族女子。他的下一步更激进的措施是命令所有官员都要讲汉语，不会讲汉语的罢官。他的这些措施引起太子的反对，以至后来当他知道太子在进行阴谋活动后，他就把太子杀了。

中国到隋代、唐代重新统一，北方的绝大多数少数民族人民都留了下来，社会上出现汉胡人民杂处现象，多民族快速融合。在唐代，大量胡人纷纷参军，单是突厥人，五品以上的将官就达到一百多人。在胡人仿效汉人生活方式的同时，汉人也兴起一股仿效胡人生活方式的热潮。首先，汉人的年轻人喜欢穿胡服，在饮食方面，从达官贵人到普通老百姓家里，用胡食招待宾客朋友，成为时尚，胡人在长安等大城市街

头开了许多酒楼餐馆，因为女主人长得漂亮，吸引了众多汉人前来光顾，这种事在史书上有不少记载，最出名的是李白的诗句，描写一帮银鞍白马的公子哥儿"落花踏尽游何处？笑入胡姬酒肆中"。此后，在魏晋南北朝时期移居中原的少数民族人民，除了有少量匈奴人跑到中亚，有一些羌族人在边远地区建立了几个羌村，其他全部都被逐步汉化，变成了汉人。

但是，长城以北的广大地区不会留下真空，当地原来少量的少数民族成长起来，数百年后又强势崛起。汉人的封建王朝到唐代达到鼎盛，唐代后期开始走下坡路，北方少数民族从宋代起就开始和汉族分庭抗礼，北宋初期，北方由契丹人建立的辽国十分强大，宋王朝倾全力和辽打了个平手，于是订立了屈辱的"澶渊之盟"，每年向辽输送大量金银物资，大宋王朝表面上繁荣昌盛，实际上风雨飘摇，所以，从宋代开始，汉族在整体政治军事力量上已经处于劣势，少数民族已经占了上风，从下面列出的朝代变化，可以清楚地看出这个发展趋势：

公元960—1127年，北宋。前期主要的敌对力量是辽国，后来，北方另一个女真族建立的金国崛起，在灭亡辽国后，于1127年突击宋朝，占领京都开封，俘虏了两个皇帝（一个是太上皇），皇亲国戚和高官们没有一个来得及逃出来，北宋灭亡，少数民族金国拥有长江以北全部疆土。

公元1127—1279年，南宋。金人进攻北宋时，皇帝有一个弟弟不在开封，他一路逃到长江以南，因为江南是水网地带，金人的骑兵难以发挥作用，惊魂方定，于是在长江以南建立一个小朝廷，定都杭州，就是南宋，国家又出现南北分治。

公元1271—1368年，元朝。少数民族蒙古族灭亡了金国和南宋皇朝，建立起一个全国性政权，这是中国第一次出现少数民族统治整个国家。蒙古族军力特别强大，成吉思汗大帝将版图扩大到中亚。

公元1368—1644年，明朝。汉族政权，封建制度江河日下，北方少数民族强敌压境，国内政治腐败，生产萧条，民不聊生，农民起义此起彼伏。

公元1644—1911年，清朝。满族人（同金人是同一个民族）征服汉人，再一次建立全国性的少数民族政权。实际上，满族统治者早已经全盘继承了汉人的政治和文化传统，所建立的政府机构和实行的规章制度和汉人的一点没有两样，他们早期的两个有名的皇帝——康熙和乾隆，都是精通国学，热爱中国古典文化，诗词文赋，样样是内行，特别是书法写得极其漂亮，可以列入历史上优秀书法家的行列。

总之，中国的两千多年历史，可以说是一部汉族和少数民族分和合、入侵和反入侵、不断地斗争和融合的历史，早期有许多少数民族已经完全融入了汉族中间，甚至像契丹这样一个曾经一度很强大的民族，现在已经完全消亡，有些民族现在改了名字，像回纥族变成回族、回纥族中一支变成维吾尔族等。

多民族融合的文化影响

新中国成立后，实现了多民族共存，政府对少数民族实行保护和扶持政策，现在中国一共有56个民族，形成一个民族大家庭。中国的多民族传统对今天的文化又有哪些影响呢？

首先在音乐舞蹈方面，后面的音乐舞蹈篇专门有一段历史上少数民族的乐器和音乐舞蹈传入到汉人地区的说明，请参阅。一直延伸到今天，少数民族大多能歌善舞，藏族姑娘嗓子高亢嘹亮，歌曲带有清亮的雪山高原色调，藏族舞蹈旋律具有鲜明特色，维吾尔族音乐舞蹈热情诙谐，带有中亚音乐韵味，蒙古族歌声抒发蓝天白云下广阔的草原情怀，他们的舞蹈彪悍奔放，其他像朝鲜族、南方的彝族、傣族、苗族等等，都有自己一方山水培育出来的各具风格的歌舞，这里不再一一叙述。

其次在服饰方面，少数民族服饰对全国影响也很大，前面说到在唐代，由于汉胡杂处，汉族男子喜欢穿胡服，女服也受胡服影响，以前汉人女服比较保守，唐代女服出现尖领、低领和袒领。到近代，因为满族统治中国数百年，现在的所谓唐装，实际上是满族服装，现在的女式旗袍，也是满族女子服装。此外，藏族等少数民族喜欢戴头饰、项链、手链等装饰品，现在带有少数民族风情的项链和手链也逐渐在全国年轻人中间流行起来。

还有在饮食方面，一千多年前，胡食曾经在汉族人中大行其道，所以今天的中国菜，尤其是北方菜，实际上已经融入了少数民族菜肴的成分。现在，当人们来到边远的少数民族地区，走进好客的少数民族人的家里，他们会端出自制的酥油茶和牛羊肉等，热情招待宾客，风味独特。此外，在北方和西北地区的城市里，还有少数民族人开的酒楼饭馆，走进饭店，会有一阵牛羊肉香味扑鼻而来。

最后谈一下建筑，中国有56个民族，由于地理、气候和风俗习惯不同，他们的房屋建筑形成也有千差万别的样式和风格。除了旅游者亲自走进少数民族地区，欣赏许

邮票上的少数民族

多华美精致的经典建筑，像布达拉宫、小布达拉宫、各种庙宇宫殿等，现在在许多城市里还专门建造了所谓的"民族村"，从北方的蒙古包到南方少数民族的民居，五花八门，还举行民族歌舞表演，供旅游者参观和了解民族风情。

Chapter 4
China's Nationalities

The Source of Ethnic Han

Chinese historians took it for granted that there existed the legendary Three Kings & Five Emperors (around 5000—2000 BC) who, in fact, were the heads of clan communities in pre-historical era. Among those kings and emperors, the most famous, one was King Yandi, also named God Farmer, living in the area of mid reaches of Yellow River in Henan Province, the other was King Huangdi, living in the area of Shaanxi and Shanxi provinces. Chinese people have regarded themselves as "Yan-Huang's descendents" because the two kings had done a lot of welfare for the people. Chinese ethnic majority also called themselves as Ethnic Han, and the word Han usually replaced the word China, such as Han people, Han language etc. The name Han was derived from the fact that the Han Dynasty (206 BC—220 AD) was the first dynasty of superpower in Chinese history.

Emperor in early dynasty

Ethnic Minorities' Invasion & Dissolve

From early time, the ethnic minorities in the north posed grave threats to Han majority in mainland for thousands of years. The minorities, being nomadic tribes, had strong military power and often made easy wealth by invading and looting Han people. Wars broke out constantly, and that became actually the matter of life or death for all Chinese dynasties through long history. But, Han society was much more developed in

37

economy and civilized in culture. As a rule, the nation less civilized would be eliminated by or assimilated into the nation that was higher civilized, and so it truly happened, the ethnic minorities were repeatedly assimilated into Han majority along with their invasions. The East Jin Dynasty (317—420) and the South & North Dynasties (420—581) saw a large-scale merging of nationalities. During the time, five powerful minorities, Xiong Nu, Xian Bei, Jie, Di, Qiang occupied most part of territory and founded 16 states successively in the north, and the Han governments could only occupy an area of south Yangtze Delta, and been assumed as small illegal regimes. But the minority rulers, after being the emperors of north China, began to call for their people to learn Han culture, studying Confucius teaching, reforming their political system and life style. Their representative figure was Emperor Xiaowendi of North Wei Dynasty, a state of ethnic Xian Bei. The ruler issued orders to press ahead great reforms: Changing their Xian Bei names into Han names, encouraging intermarriage between Xian Bei and Han people, even more, he ordered all of his officials to speak Han language, and removing those who didn't speak. His extreme policies had provoked the defiance of his son, the crown prince, and he finally killed his son.

In Sui (581—618) and Tang (618—709) dynasties, China was unified again, when a large number of minority people had preferred to stay in the mainland, and they were called as "Hu". During Tang, a lot of Hu youth joined the army and there show up many famous Hu military commanders. In capital Changan City (now Xi'an, Shaanxi Province) , Han young people liked to wear Hu clothes, Han families from high level officials to the grass roots liked to eat Hu food, or to hold Hu food feasts to serve their guests as a vogue. There also were many Hu food restaurants on Chang'an streets, and the smile of young and pretty Hu proprietress had solicited many Han loyal customers. After hundreds of years, all the Hu people had dissolved or be assimilated into Han nationality.

But in the vast area outside the Great Wall, the new ethnic minorities had soon risen up. In early Song Dynasty (around 1000 AD), a minority Liao State shared an equal military power with Song, and forced Song government to sign a giving-in agreement. As a matter of fact, China's feudal civilization and military power reached its climax in Tang Dynasty, and began stepping downward from the mid Tang. In other words, from then on, the military power of northern minorities did surpass that of Han dynasties. Following were the names of later dynasties listed in order:

In 1127, Jin State, another northern minority power, after conquering Liao State, encircled and captured Kaifen, Song's capital in Henan Province, only one of the emperor's brothers who was not in Kaifen, escaped southward and founded a mall regime in Yangtze Delta, the South Song Dynasty, and made its capital in Hangzhou, Zhejiang Province. Historians, therefore, divided Song Dynasty into North Song and

South Song dynasties.

In 1271, Mongolians, after conquering both Jin State and South Song, founded an unified country Yuan Dynasty (1271—1368). Mongolians boasted to have extraordinary powerful troops, and Genghis Khan The Great had made China's territory far stretching to mid Asia.

In 1368, ethnic Han founded Ming Dynasty (1368—1644).

In 1644, ethnic minority Manchu founded Qing Dynasty (1644—1911), the last feudal dynasty of China, and it inherited all Ming's political and cultural traditions.

In 1911, the revolution led by Dr. Sun Yeh Sen overthrew Qing Dynasty.

In a word, China's history over thousands of years has been a history of separating and merging between Han majority and many minority nationalities.

Cultural Effects of Multi-Nationalities

After the founding of the new China, the government issued policies to help and protect the people of ethnic minorities. Now China is home to people of 56 nationalities, becoming a big family of multi-nationality country, and the special situation had featured a multi-nationality culture, such as:

Firstly, there are a variety of ethnic minorities' music and dance displaying their characteristic features respectively. (See detailed explanation in chapter 12) Every ethnic minority autonomous region now have their singing & dancing troupes, bringing their different styles and flavors of folk arts on the stages all around the country. The troupes also go abroad performing on the stages of international carnivals.

People of ethnic minorities have the traditions of clothing and personal adornments of their own. (See detailed explanation in chapter 15) The minorities' clothes had brought about great impacts to Chinese clothing culture in history. Up-to-date, some of minorities' clothing and adornments like Tang clothes and Tibetan necklace and bracelet still come into fashion nation-wide.

The present day Chinese food had already absorbed the cream of minorities' cuisine in

Patron Gods of Han people

Tang Dynasty. (See detailed explanation in chapter 13) Now, minorities people still have their own diet tastes traditions. When coming into their eateries, travelers could smell strong aroma of beef or lam with special spices.

The architecture of ethnic minorities has now become the resources for developing tourism industry. China has a vast territory and different natural conditions in the north and south, that forming a variety of ways of styles and structures of people's residences. Now in some hot tourist resorts, there appear a kind of "multi-nationalities architecture museum", spotlighting a new attraction for travelers.

文学（上）

上古文学

　　中国的古文从它一开始就出现两个辉煌的高峰，一个在春秋战国时期（公元前770—前221年），一个在汉代（公元前206—公元220年）。作为古文的基本文体，记叙文、散文和韵文，这两座高峰后世文学家再也没有能够超越。春秋战国时期的古文主要有两类：一是思想家们的学术著作，"文以载道"，像孔子的《论语》和由他修订的几部经典，孟、老、庄、墨以及诸子百家著作，这些著作文字一般很大气，有理论高度，思想锐利，语言精辟，所以成了中国第一批文学瑰宝。第二类是历史传记文，当时周朝王室和各诸侯国都有专门的史官，把国家大事都记录下来，这批作品叙人光彩熠熠，记事曲折生动，许多名篇千年来脍炙人口。当然，中国最早的诗歌《诗经》和楚辞也是诞生在这个时期。汉代掀起第二个文学高潮，实际上是春秋时期文学高峰的延续，出现一批名垂史册的史学家、政论家、辞赋家的不朽作品。

郑玄读书图

唐　诗

　　喜欢写诗大概是中华民族的天性。中国最早的一部

李白画像

诗集是《诗经》，在那个年代居然能收集到这么多丰富的民歌，艺术品位也很高，是个奇迹。《诗经》里的诗是四言诗，就是每句四个字（五言诗就是每句五字，类推），而到了汉代，五言诗流行起来。从汉到魏晋南北朝的八百多年时间里，诗歌创作蓬勃发展，出现了大批著名诗人和在诗歌史上熠熠生辉的不朽作品。

唐诗，就是在这样的温暖气候和肥沃土壤里开放出的一朵特别鲜艳的奇葩，它也是世界文学宝库里的一颗明珠。

整个唐代（公元618—907年）到底有多少诗人，创作了多少诗歌，现在无法估计，经过大量散失，今天留有姓名的诗人还有二千二百多人，留下的诗歌大约十万九千首。唐诗发展分初唐、盛唐、中唐和晚唐四个时期。盛就是繁荣，盛唐时期无论是诗人的人数，还是诗歌的数量和水平，都达到了最高峰。杜甫和李白是两颗最耀眼的明星，后人称杜甫为"诗圣"，称李白为"诗仙"。杜诗多描写社会动乱和人民疾苦，风格深沉雄放，人们赞誉他的一支笔"力摧五岳，气扫三军"，他自己也说自己"读书破万卷，下笔如有神"，所以他的诗被称为"史诗"。李白天赋过人，才华横溢，一生藐视权贵而放荡不羁，痛恨社会黑暗而饮酒浇愁，他的诗想象纵横驰骋，语言洒脱奔放。就四个时期而言，除杜甫和李白处在无可争议的高度外，每个时期大约有二三十个诗人可能处在同一个水平上，他们个个都是大手笔、大诗豪，个个都有传世的经典诗作和自己的特色，给后人留下一份厚重的遗产。目前唐诗的读本很多，在适合一般读者的普及版中，由清代蘅塘退士编的《唐诗三百首》是一部比较理想的选本，所选诗都是千百年来经过历史筛选的最精华的作品，当然也有不足，一是为了照顾诗人间平衡，许多好诗遗留在外。再是选了大量长诗，虽然它们也是最高境界的精品，但初学者读起来会感到困难。

诗歌，人们用来倾诉和抒发内心的感情。唐诗的数量大，内容自然也十分丰富。诗人在日常生活中遇到即兴灵感，眼前的偶发事件，或在旅行途中触景生情，往往就

蒲湖白雨斜拖脚水面抛珠乱入船着雨看山还自得何须着屐学披仙　沈周

雨中吟诗图

会咏一首诗将它们表达出来，所以唐诗里有大量的"偶书"、"漫兴"之类作品。但唐诗的内容远远超出了一般个人的喜怒哀乐，而是深入地反映了社会现象和文化特点，主要是：第一，盛唐后期发生了一次大规模军阀叛乱，即安史之乱（安禄山和史思明），战火延烧了大半个中国，京城长安（今陕西省西安市）陷落，皇帝逃到四川，繁荣昌盛、歌舞升平的世界，一下变成人间地狱，国内许多地方呈现千村万落不见人烟、十室九空的凄惨景象。诗歌对这一历史现象作了真实的记录；第二，唐代在边境和少数民族的战事一直不断，盛唐中有不少诗人跟随部队到边疆，亲自经历军旅生活，写出了一批反映边疆战争的诗歌，极其雄浑悲壮。后世诗评家把这类诗称为边塞诗，称这一类诗人为边塞派诗人；第三，有一部分知识分子长期安家在山野，过着隐居生活，他们从各个方面歌颂大自然的美丽，抒发自己心灵和自然相通的感情。这些诗的艺术性达到很高的境界，诗评家称它们为田园诗，称这些诗人为田园派诗人；第四，中国古典诗歌还有一个重要内容，就是评论或歌颂某一历史事件或人物，或是议论一种社会现象，可以称为议论诗。诗人写这类诗时，往往目光独到，寥寥几个字就把事件的本质深刻地揭露出来；第五，中国知识分子重视友谊，他们写了大量的离别诗和怀念诗。这类诗歌不但感情真挚，艺术性高，而且也成为后人研究他们的重要材料。

最后，唐诗在形式上也有很大变化，更加趋于成熟。唐代诗人写诗分为古体诗和今体诗两大类，古体诗指在唐代以前就已经存在和流行的诗体，五言的或七言的，长短不等。这里着重说一说今体诗，就是格律诗，这是唐代新流行起来的一种主流诗体。格律诗简单地说有两点：一是两个固定，固定了每句句子的字数，五字或七字，同时固定了每首诗的句子数，四句或八句。四句诗称为"绝"，五字的是五绝，七字的是七绝；八句诗称为"律"，五字的是五律，七字的是七律。就是说，一共只有五绝、七绝、五律、七律四种形式，很好记。二是不论绝和律，全诗都要讲究四声，也就是平仄声，当然也讲韵脚。四种形式都有规定的平仄谱。由于这方面比较专业，说起来也繁琐，这里就略去不谈。

格律诗有什么好处呢？因为它短，内容就精简浓缩，因为它讲四声，念起来就抑扬顿挫，更有韵味，因此，它就具备了其他诗所没有的最大长处：易诵易记，易于推广。唐诗被人们广泛传诵，得到空前普及，它的格律化起了很大的作用。同时，格律诗模式，也被以后朝代的诗人代代继承下来。

宋 词

苏辙像

在唐诗的高峰面前，后世无法超过，于是宋代（公元960—1279年）兴起了"词"。词也是古典诗歌的一种，诗和词在翻译成外文时简直无法区别，但实际上它们的差别还是很大的。在形式上，格律诗只有五绝、七绝、五律、七律四种样式，古体诗虽然句子不限，但文字和句子的长短都很整齐。而词则分为各种词调，每种词调的句子多少和长短都不一样。词调冠有各种名称，像《望江南》、《虞美人》、《浣溪沙》、《念奴娇》等等，有一百多种。词对文字四声和韵律的要求更为严格，这是因为当时它们都是配上固定的乐曲，适合人们吟唱的。由于每种词调都规定好字数和四声，好像一份表格，写词就像填表格，所以叫"填词"。

唐诗和宋词的另外一个显著差别表现在内容、风格和精神上。这一点在这里用简单几句话讲不清楚，概括起来可以这样说，唐诗一般讲求豪迈铿锵的气势，而宋词则表现清丽婉约的情调。不过还应当确切地说，宋词的主流是婉约，婉约派的词人和他们的作品，占了全部宋词的大多数，但另有几个豪放派词人，他们人数虽少，但作品艺术成就极高、影响极大，代表人物就是苏轼和辛弃疾。婉约派有个著名词人名叫柳永，据说有井的地方，就是有人居住的地方，就会有人唱他的词。有一天，苏轼问他一个朋友，他的词和柳永的词比起来怎样？朋友说，柳永的词适合十五六岁小姑娘，用樱桃小口细细吟唱，而你的词适合彪形关西大汉，用大嗓子，拿一根铁棍子打着节拍唱。这几句话很形象，三言两语说清楚了婉约派和豪放派词的区别。

元 曲

到了元代（公元1271—1368年）出现了"曲"的诗歌形式。曲是从词演变过来的，开始没有和戏剧结合时，叫散曲。和词一样，每首散曲有曲名，也有固定的音

《元曲选》中的插图

《元人杂剧选》中的插图

乐。而曲和词的不同点是，曲的内容更加生活化，用字更加口语，用韵也不像诗和词那样严格，只要发音相似就可以了。特别是曲可以在规定的句子以外，临时添加"衬字"，譬如加"啊呀"、"天哪"之类的字帮助语气，添字有时候可以多达十几个字。后来，散曲渐渐和戏剧相结合。这一方面是由于沿海一带许多城市兴起，带动戏曲繁盛起来，同时，元朝是由蒙古族统治，他们取消科举，知识分子断了做官的道路，就把注意力转到戏曲创作方面来。所以后来人们所说的元曲，就是指在舞台上表演的歌剧，它也是中国传统戏曲的起源。元代出现了许多重量级戏曲艺术家，以及他们创作的传世经典作品，几个著名的元曲作家的名字，和唐代最著名的诗人、宋代最著名的词人一起，在中国文学史上放出永恒的光辉。

Chapter 5
Literature (Part 1)

Early Literature

Chinese early literature creation reached its peak for two times, one was as early as in the Spring & Autumn Period and the Warring States Period, (770—221 BC) and the other was in Han Dynasty (206 BC—220 AD). The literature in the Spring & Autumn and the Warring States periods consisted mainly of two forms: One was the works of ancient great philosophers and scholars, such as Confucius, Laozi, Mozi, and other scholars, that became China's earliest literary treasures, and the other was the prose describing historical matters and persons, written by the officials especially responsible for recording down important historical stories. This part of prose also became classical literary masterpieces due to their high literary values. The Han Dynasty saw the second peak of literature creation. During the dynasty, a lot of men of letters, historians, political commentators and rhythmical prose writers showed up, and their works also became the essence of classics of Chinese literature. In fact, the works produced in the two peaks had been regarded to be not only the foundation of Chinese literature but the source of Chinese early civilization. They had never been surmounted in later generations.

Tang Poetry

Composing poetry had probably been the nature of Chinese people. China's earliest poetry anthology came into being during the Spring & Autumn Period named *Shi Jing* (literally Poetry Bible) compiled by Confucius himself. In late Warring States Period, there came forth the great poet Qü Yuan and his lengthy poem *Woe on Departure*. And during the following 800 years from Han Dynasty to the South & North Dynasties Period, numerous poets composed a lot of classics of poetry masterpieces providing the fertile soil and fine weather for the abundant growth of Tang poetry.

In Tang Dynasty (618—907) China's classical poetry creation reached its peak, and there were some 39,000 poems made by some 2,200 poets passed down up-to-date. Tang poetry was a special brilliant pearl in the treasury house of Chinese literature, as

Poet Du Fu

well as one of the greatest culture heritages in human history.

Poetry is a kind of feeling passion voiced out from people's inner mind. Tang poets have composed many poems inspired by a variety of events from their day-to-day life, but the subject matter of Tang poetry went far from the limitation of depicting poets' individual weal and woe:

1. In the prosperous period of mid Tang, there broke out a nationwide violence war launched by two powerful warlords named An and Shi, (The An Shi Rebellion was an important incident in Chinese history) and people's peaceful life all of a sudden fell down into a terrible hell. The great poet Du Fu and other poets depicted full of the disastrous scenes in their works.

2. There were frequent border wars broke out between ethnic Han and minorities troops. Many intellectuals went to the border or joined the military, and composed a lot of poems depicting remote and desolate mountains and rivers as well as bloody battles with the special rhythms of wilderness and magnificence. Critics named this kind of poetry as "the border poetry".

3. There were a number of poets who shut themselves off from everyday world and led a secluded life in desolated countryside or deep mountains. They depicted the natural beauty in their poems, or even showing their soles being dissolved into the wide of universe. Critics named this kind of poetry as "the idyll poetry".

4. Another kind of poetry could be named as "the commentary poetry." When some poets visited a historical ruin, or came across a special social phenomenon, they would speak out their views, usually penetrating, precise and distinct, by composing a poem.

5. As Chinese intellectuals liked to make friends and valued highly to their friendship, they made a great deal of poems, saying goodbye or missing their friends, that could be named as "the friendship poetry".

In addition to the subject matters and contents, the forms of Chinese classical poetry had also experienced a significant change in Tang Dynasty, mainly featuring so-called "metrical poetry", i.e., 1. the number of line was fixed, only having four lines or eight lines; 2. the number of letter in every lines was also fixed, only having five letters or seven letters; 3. there were fixed tone for most of the letters (Chinese letters have divided four different tones) , helping poems to be more harmonious in tones and rhymes. Tang poets also have composed a huge amount of non-metrical poetry, (mostly lengthy poems) named "ancient-formed poetry", indicating the difference between two forms of poetry. But, the new form "metrical poetry" made the poems to be easier to read, easier to memorize, easier to popularize, and finally made easier for them pass down generation by generation.

The Tang poetry, as being explained above, was not only a lavishing beautiful flower of Chinese culture, but also a great treasure house itself containing a wide range of historical and cultural connotations. But in current editions of Tang poetry anthologies, the explanations of the poems were usually too short and simple, and more, as a tradition, their cultural connotations have almost been ignored. Zhou Ji, the autor of this book, had written another work *Pearls of Tang & Song Poetry — with English and Chinese expressions* which put special stress on delving into indepth connotations of the poems, so when people read the poems, they could also learn a lot of interesting stories, including politics, social customs, culture, people's lifestyle and ideology.

Song Ci-Poetry

Being faced the insurmountable artistic peak of Tang poetry, intellectuals in Song Dynasty (960—1279) developed a new style of poetry named ci-poetry. Though Tang poetry and ci-poetry are both Chinese classical poetry, but there are some significant differences between them. One of the most notable difference was their forms: The form of Tang poetry was simple and unified, while ci-poetry had a variety of forms called "ci-brand". There were hundred different ci-brands. Each of ci-brand had its different name, different number of words and lines. Especially, they were all set to fixed music, just like songs sung popularly among the people. Another difference between Tang poetry and ci-poetry was their taste and spirit, but it was hard to explain clearly in a few words. Generally speaking, Tang poetry displayed sonorous rhyme and strong momentum, while ci-poetry displayed sweet tone and delicate taste. People could only make sense of the differences after they have learned and compared a certain amount of both kinds of poetry by themselves.

Yuan Drama

In Yuan Dynasty (1271—1368), ci-poetry began to give way to "qü" (both meaning song and drama). In Yuan, along with the development of cities and towns and the

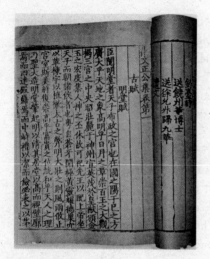

A book written by Yuan scholar

ever increasing of entertaining demands of city residents, the stage performing art became into vogue, a fact that inspired intellectuals turning their efforts to create stage plays. They integrated individual qü into drama, and actually made china's stage drama to be some kind of opera. So, qü was also a kind of China's classical poetry, and some of qü works written by renowned qü artists had been highly valued and admired through centuries.

《红楼梦》

《红楼梦》不但列为四大古典小说之首，而且是中国数千年文学史上的一座丰碑。它在清代乾隆中期（公元1760年前后）问世后，立即引起轰动，许多人称它为奇书。奇者，高深莫测也，因此出现许多专门研究《红楼梦》的学者，这一专门学科称为"红学"，研究者称为"红学家"，奇书的作者曹雪芹也成了研究的对象。两个半世纪来，红学家们一批一批出现，人们从各个角度研究，但正像鲁迅所说，经学家看到《易》，道学家看到淫，流言学家看到宫闱秘事。好像一个大树林，里面什么鸟都有。近代的新红学鼻祖胡适说，他研究红学是为了好玩。这好玩两字说得非常到位，因为书里面不但有许多活灵活现的人物，还有建筑、园林、绘画、美食，以及诗、词、曲、赋等，文化内涵无所不包，使人越看越有味道。现在红学家遍及全世界，国际红学会还定期举行研讨会，中国有哪一本书会走红到这个程度？没有。甚至有一位红学家语出惊人：中国可以没有万里长城，但是不可以没有《红楼梦》，这话还真有一定的道理。

《红楼梦》中的"大观园"

以下对这部巨著分四部

分作最简要的介绍。

一、《红楼梦》故事梗概。小说的故事发生在清代早期，描写一个高级官僚家庭，从极端富贵到衰败破亡的过程。男主人公贾宝玉出生时嘴里含着一块玉，因而名叫宝玉。女主人公黛玉是宝玉的表妹，贾府聚集着十二个聪慧秀美的女孩，春夏秋冬成天做些吟诗玩乐的事情。宝玉和黛玉互相一见钟情，但另有个秀外慧中、贤淑出众的姑娘宝钗，进入了竞争角色。因为黛玉性格孤傲，且疾病缠身，贾家上上下下逐渐有意拆散宝黛，而促成宝玉和宝钗的婚姻。当宝玉和宝钗成婚之夜，宝玉还以为面前的新娘是黛玉，而这时黛玉正当垂死之际，她听到了远远传来的鼓乐声。贾家最后被朝廷惩罚，抄没家产，宝玉出家做了和尚。

《红楼梦》影印版

二、《红楼梦》描写一个社会。《红楼梦》的故事情节并不复杂，而是用细腻笔调描写一个个生动的生活场景，把一幅庞大绚丽的社会和生活画卷呈现在读者面前。在当地，贾家和另外史、王、薛家，四个家族的势力霸占一方，欺压百姓，贾府里的人男盗女娼，各个利益集团的人互相明争暗斗，先后冤枉死了几十条人命。整个家族生活靡费，连年入不敷出，不久皇帝下令惩罚贾家，抄家后没收财产，大树轰然倒地，林鸟纷纷凄惨逃命。贾家的覆亡反映了封建社会权力斗争的内部规律。

三、《红楼梦》的艺术成就。《红楼梦》重点描写的是人。莎士比亚在他全部的戏剧作品中创作了近一百个人物形象，而曹雪芹在《红楼梦》前八十回里，也创造了近一百个艺术形象，描绘细致入微，笔触生动流畅，每个人的音容笑貌和行为举止都有鲜明的个性，有几十个人鲜活得似乎要从纸上走下来。大家公认，《红楼梦》的人物描写，不愧是空前绝后的大手笔。

四、《红楼梦》里的诗歌。《红楼梦》前八十回有大量的诗歌，艺术水平达到传统诗歌的巅峰（曹雪芹写了前八十回就贫病去世，后四十回由高鹗续写完成，两部分水平有明显差距，尤其是诗歌，高鹗显然表现技穷）。小说里有格律诗、长诗，有词，还有散曲，其中许多作品字字玑珠，句句警策，意境高逸，妙趣横生，寓意深刻，特别是每首诗歌风格都和作者（书中人物）个性完全符合，其艺术成就直追唐、宋、元一些最著名的大师。曹雪芹自己对这些诗歌也是很欣赏和得意的。

《三国演义》

《三国演义》是讲发生在三国时代（公元220—280年）的故事，作者罗贯中（1330—1400年）。东汉末年，天下大乱，军阀混战，群雄四起，后来由三位英雄建立起三个独立国家，形成鼎立局面。这是中国历史上一个非常特殊的时代，三方进行错综复杂的军事、政治和外交斗争，这样的历史条件必然要演绎许多精彩故事，造就许多著名英雄。这段历史另有一部官方正史《三国志》，而《三国演义》是小说，作者把人物和故事都加以典型化、理想化，使主要人物的形象更鲜明，故事更富有情趣魅力，因此一直受到广大人民喜爱，书中的许多独立故事，都被京剧和其他地方剧种编成保留节目反复演出，可以说没有任何一个朝代像三国时期那样，有这么多故事和

赤壁大战（年画）

英雄人物的名字深入人心，家喻户晓。

下面把三个国家分别作简要介绍。

魏国　地域包括长江以北的广大中原地区，人口众多，经济发达，君主曹操，兵多将广，是三国中最强大的一方。曹操囚禁皇帝，把持朝政，他儿子废汉建立魏国，并追认他为魏武帝。由于篡夺皇位被认为是大逆不道，加上他为人凶险奸诈，小说把他描写成头号坏蛋，但事实上曹操是个高明的政治家、军事家，在诗歌创作上也有辉煌成就。曹操死后历史重演，魏国的军事统帅司马懿也逼魏主让位，司马家族先后灭亡三国，建立晋朝，重新统一中国。

蜀国　地据长江中上游和四川省一带，国君刘备。《三国演义》一开头就讲刘备和关羽、张飞三人结拜成兄弟一起参军，就是"桃园三结义"的故事。关羽的故事很多，他在极端困难条件下，矢志不渝地效忠刘备。所以关羽被后世树为"忠义"典型，在全国各地造起"关帝庙"，每年举行祭祀，关羽的知名度在广大乡村甚至超过孔子。但蜀国还有第一号英雄诸葛亮，小说浓墨重彩描写诸葛亮料事如神、克敌制胜的故事，诸葛亮的名字成了中华民族智慧的化身。诸葛亮有一句话也很有名，即"鞠躬尽瘁，死而后已"，他后来因劳累死在军中。

吴国　地拥长江中下游广大区域，占气候、物产等地理优势。国君孙权，他从父兄手里接过统治权时，年方二十出头。有一次他和曹操两军对阵，曹操看到他身边猛将如云，前呼后拥，赞叹说："生子当如孙仲谋（仲谋是孙权的字）。"小说里讲吴国故事最多的，一个是前期大元帅周瑜，他联合蜀国，以弱胜强，赤壁一战打败曹操军马，奠定了三国鼎立的局面。后期，吴国军队偷袭并杀死蜀大将关羽，刘备倾兵讨伐吴国为关羽报仇，吴国一位年轻儒将陆逊以弱势坚守阵地，最后火烧蜀军连营八百里而取得胜利。

《水　浒》

北宋（960—1127年）后期，国家政治腐败，贪官污吏横行，生产凋敝，民不聊生。山东省境内有一座四面环水的山林——梁山泊，一批"盗寇"在这里啸聚，劫富济贫，打击官府，与朝廷抗衡，这便是小说《水浒》的梗概。梁山"盗寇"的首领名叫宋江，史书记载确有宋江等36人起义，但很快就被镇压下去。早先，《水浒》里的许多独立故事，在民间的演剧和说书场所广为流传，到元末明初，小说家施耐庵（约1296—1370年）把分散的故事串连起来，编写成这部长篇巨著。封建社会里许多事情合法不合理，或合理不合法，由于故事来自民间，老百姓在这里选择了自己的是非和爱憎，表达了自己的愿望，因此，《水浒》的最大特点是把官方的正统观念和法律标准颠倒过来，成为合理即合法，大盗也有道，这些"盗寇"原本都是英雄好汉，书中所写的所有投奔梁山的人，追究起来都是由于政府压迫造成，是"逼上梁山"，所有看起来杀人不眨眼的豪强身上，都有一股正义的英雄气概。关于这点，英国作家亨利·吉尔柏写的小说《罗宾汉》，其立场和《水浒》正如出一辙。

《西 游 记》

《西游记》是一部神怪小说，讲唐朝一位高僧到西天取经的故事，作者吴承恩（约1500—1582年）。西天取经确有其事，唐僧原型叫陈玄奘，他花了17年时间，到印度取来佛经六百多部，而且在印度学会梵文（印度古文），回国后把佛经翻译出来。当时他从长安（今陕西省西安市）出发，到新疆后再南下，徒步行走，穿越茫茫沙漠和高山大川，经历了难以想象的险阻，表现出超乎常人的毅力，因此，后来写成的小说《西游记》就被荒诞化了。去西天取经的团伙一共师徒四人，不过，在这里唐僧被描写成糊涂怯懦，一遇到危险只会发抖念菩萨救命的老好人。唐僧的这种性格正好突出他的徒弟孙悟空（猴王），他本领高强，上天入地，威名远播，一路降妖伏魔，在取经过程中立了第一功。唐僧另外两个徒弟猪八戒和沙和尚本事平平，但也有鲜明性格，像猪八戒好吃懒做，爱搬弄是非，每次看到女人还要忘乎所以；沙僧对取经忠心耿耿，挑一副沉重行李始终是他的分内活。

其 他

《金瓶梅》 由于在书里有大量露骨的性描写，它一直被列为禁书。不过评论家们对这部小说的评价很高，主要因为它是第一部直接描写平民阶层生活的小说，记录了宋代社会大量的民间生活习俗，对后人了解历史有很大意义。作者"兰陵笑笑生"是个笔名，明代人。

《儒林外史》 儒林指读书人，外史是传说，合起来意思就是读书人的故事，基本上是对读书人进行讽刺和嘲笑。作者吴敬梓。全书没有统一结构，说完一个人再说一个人，相互也没有关系。书中最著名的一个故事是"范进中举"，说范进考了几十年举人，到五十多岁才"中举"，他听到消息后突然发疯了。杜甫诗"儒冠多误身"，信哉。

《聊斋志异》 是一部短篇小说集，大部分讲狐狸精和鬼魂等荒诞故事，但这些鬼怪一点也不吓人，相反倒是善良可亲，讨人喜欢，有些故事几乎妇孺皆知。小说用文言文体，但描写极为活泼生动，文字极有灵气光彩。作者蒲松龄。

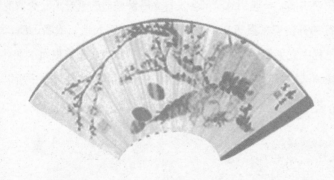

Chapter 6
Literature (Part 2), Four Classical Novels

Dream of Red Mansion

The novel *Dream of Red Mansion*, written by Cao Xueqin, was a glorious monument of Chinese literature. As soon as it came forth in early Qing Dynasty (around 1760), it was acclaimed nationwide as a "strange book". The word "strange" meant "too deep to probe the bottom". The book described vividly the natures of a variety of people, as well as architectures, gardens, cuisine, arts, poetry and all of cultural elements, that provoking many scholars to make research of it. The research course was named as "Red Course", and the scholars were named "Red Course Scholars". For more than two centuries, red course scholars came out generation by generation, but, things turned out that the more the researches they made, the more profound the book seemed to be. Now, red course symposiums are held every two or three years attended by the red scholars came from both mainland China and overseas, and they claimed they always made new discoveries when making researches from different angles. One of the red course scholars even made his remarks startlingly: The novel *Dream of Red Mansion* is more important than the Great Wall for China.

The story of the novel set in the early years of Qing Dynasty. The two young protagonists, Bao Yu and Dai Yu, fell in love with each other at first sight in their early tens. Bao Yu, (literally meaning precious jade) born into a high official family. He kept a piece of jade in his mouth when he was born, the fact his name was derived from. Dai Yu, a pretty and clever girl and a cousin of Bao Yu, lived with his family. The rich and big family was homed to 12 pretty young girls who led their happy life by composing poems, making literally games and other amusements. But, due to Dai Yu's aloof and uncompanionable disposition and her questionable health, Bao Yu's parents finally gave up her and turned to an alternative Bao Chai, a gentle and kind girl, to be Bao Yu' wife. In the wedding evening, Bao Yu still believed the bride was Dai Yu, who, however, at the moment lying on her dying bed, heard the festive wedding music in the distance spread into her ears. Afterwards, Bao Yu's official father was dismissed by the emperor, and their properties were all been confiscated. The large tree fell in a sudden, and the birds hanging-on dispersed in panic. Bao Yu finally left his family and became a Buddhist monk.

Dream of Red Mansion offered a true and spectacular picture scroll of feudal society through vivid and exquisite description, especially, portraying successfully more than 100 figures with their living and distinct characteristic natures. Also, there were a lot of poems in the novel, including poems, lengthy poems, ci-poems, qü-poems. The literary value of the poems could match that of the masterpieces made by most famous poets and top literary giants in Tang, Song and Yuan dynasties.

Tales of Three Kingdoms

The tales set in the Three Kingdoms Period (220—280). In the chaotic years of late Han Dynasty, people riots broke out, and the armed warlords fought each other to expand their territory. At last, there left three most powerful warlords occupied three parts of territory and founded three independent states, resulting in the appearance of the new Period replacing Han Dynasty. The three kingdoms were.

Wei Kingdom, occupied the most developed and densely-populated area of mid and north China, was the most powerful state among the three. The emperor of Wei, Cao Cao, due to be described in the novel as a wicked evildoer, left behind his stinking name for thousands of years. But, in reality, he was a capable politician and strategist as well as a great man of letters in Chinese history. After Cao's death, his military commander Sima Yi overthrew Wei and other two states, founded a new unified country, Jin Dynasty.

Shu Kingdom, occupied the area of upper reaches of Yangtze River and Sichuan Province, took the advantages of having talented officials and valorous generals. Zhuge Liang, Shu' premier and the most outstanding wise man in the novel, was regarded to be the symbol of intelligence and wisdom of Chinese nationality. Guan Yu, a Shu's military commander had also won a household name as he behaved extremely loyal and honest to the emperor, also his sworn brother Liu Bei. Guan's name was even more popular than Confucius among households in northern countryside.

A scene from *Tales of Three Kingdoms*

Wu Kingdom, occupied the mid and lower reaches of Yangtze River, boasted to have geographical advantages as well as powerful army.

The Three Kingdoms Period was a special stage in Chinese history, featuring intricate military, political and diplomatic struggles among three parties, producing lots of intriguing stories and many famous heroes. Many stories in the novel had long been adapted into dramas, operas and other entertaining programs that made the stories and heroes much more popular through centuries. The novelist was Luo Guanzhong (1330—1400).

Outlaws in Marshland

In late Song Dynasty, people lived in dire poverty, and corrupted officials forced people to rise up or forced them to be "robbers" and "bandits". There were 108 violent outlaws occupied Liangshan Marshland in Shandong Province, robbing the rich and helping the poor, and defying government troops. The stories about outlaws were firstly written separately by some folk artists into plays performing on stages for hundreds of years, and finally were summed up by the novelist Shi Nai'an (1296—1376) into a lengthy

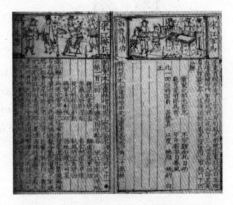

Outlaws in Marshland

novel. Due to the stories were come from grassroots, people displayed views of their own, creating their own criterion of right and wrong. In the novel the killers and rioters were praised as savers or heroes, and the government officials were criticized as evildoers.

A Trip to West

It was a novel of mythology, written by Wu Cheng'en (1500—1582). The novel depicted the Monkey King, a half immortal hero with great magic arts, escorting his Buddhist master Tang Monk to go to the west (India) , to acquire Buddhist sutras. Monkey King was a household name, and the stories of "Monkey King Made Big Scenes at Heaven Palace" and "Monkey King Attacked White Skeleton Demon for Three Times" were specially popular and never lost its appeal among the people.

Other Novels

Jinpingmei (literally meaning golden jar plum) was the first of the kind depicting in

The Monkey King in opera make-up

vivid and in details of society and people's day-to-day life in Song Dynasty, so it was praised highly by critics and historians. But it was banned to the public because there were a lot of descriptions of sex activities in the book. The author was "Lanlin Laughing And Laughing Man", a pen name.

Complementary Stories of Intellectuals, written by Wu Jinzi was mainly dealt with different types of behaviors of Confucius disciples with criticizing and satiric tones.

Liaozhai's Queer Stories, written by Pu Songling, was a short-story collection mostly dealt with stories related to the fox demons and ghosts. They were usually transfigured into pretty girls and seemed lovely and kind-minded, instead of giving people horrible feelings.

对联和中国文字

中国文字是一个个方块子，一个字一个音节，这个特点必然会产生对联这个形式。所谓对联，就是两句字数相等的句子，双方所排列的字，它们的意思正好相对称，动物对动物，天体对天体，数字对数字，颜色对颜色，虚字对虚字等，所以也叫对仗句。例如：

　　　五月黄梅天　　　　三星白兰地

这里五对三，月对星，黄对白，梅对兰，天对地。

再例如杜甫诗句：

　　　两个黄鹂鸣翠柳　　　一行白鹭上青天

上面句子里，两个对一行，黄鹂对白鹭，鸣对上（飞上），翠柳对青天。

这里要同时指出，中国文字有四声区别，第一和第二声属平声，第三和第四声属仄声，两句里相对称的字平仄要相反，尤其是第二、第四、第六字，像上句：个是仄，行是平，鹂是平，鹭是仄，翠是仄，青是平，当然，最后一个字最重要，柳是仄，天是平。

以上是关于对联的基本概念。也可以说，对联是中国文字的高一级形式，是文学的一部分，它表

对联

现中国文字的形象美、结构美和音律美，所以学中文一定要懂对联，会欣赏对联，至少要知道一些对联知识。

对联在春秋时期的《诗经》里就有了，像"行迈靡靡，中心摇摇"（一个人走路摇摇晃晃，心情恍惚迷茫）和"投我以木桃，报之以琼瑶"（投桃报李的意思）等。战国后期出现的楚辞，汉代出现的赋，使用对仗句更多了。南北朝盛行一种骈体文，整篇文章全部用对仗句写成，每句四字或六字，也叫四六文，当时风气是，不是四六文，不算好文章。因为骈体文只追求文字华美，内容言之无物，所谓以文害义，所以到唐代逐渐消失，唐诗代而兴起。

唐诗宋词和对联

唐诗也是突出对仗句的，看杜甫一首著名的《登高》：

风急天高猿啸哀，渚清沙白鸟飞回。

无边落木萧萧下，不尽长江滚滚来。

万里悲秋常作客，百年多病独登台。

艰难苦恨繁霜鬓，潦倒新停浊酒杯。

上面一首诗共八句（叫律诗），可以看到，它的中间四句，即第三和第四句是对仗句，第五和第六句也是对仗句，凡是唐诗八句的律诗，当中的四句必然是对仗句，这是一个重要规则。四句的诗（绝诗）没有对仗规定，但是许多诗里还是有对仗句，上面提到的"两个黄鹂鸣翠柳"两句就是例子。宋词里的对仗句也很多，哪些句子必须相对，也是规定好的。唐宋诗词并没有以文害义，相反，里面精彩的对联成千上万，美不胜收，有许多对联自然天成，像是诗人灵感来时创作起来毫不费力，其实不然，他们往往为了想一个字，连续几天几夜捻胡子抓头皮，废寝忘食。这里有个有趣故事：宋代大词人晏殊的"无可奈何花落去，似曾相识燕归来"一联十分有名，据说他开始先想到下句"似曾相识燕归来"，想上句却难住了。他有一个习惯，把不成熟的句子写在一张纸条上，贴在书房墙上，便于思考，但还是连续几个月想不出对句。后来有一天有个朋友来访，看到纸条，想了一会，说："无可奈何花落去"怎样？晏殊眼前突然一亮，大喜过望，于是他就写出了千古名作《浣溪沙》。所以，对联和诗词两者相辅相成，结成了特殊的关系，对联极大地增强了诗词的光彩、魅力和韵味，而诗词反过来扩大了对联的影响。唐诗宋词念的人多，学龄儿童都要念，万口传诵，几千年来，对联能够如此广泛深入地流传于人民生活之中，这可以说完全得益于诗词的推广普及。

对联无处不在

关于对联，在人们日常生活中，首先应该提到春联。每当春节来临，家家户户迎来万象更新，纷纷把陈旧的褪了色的春联取下，换上新的鲜红的春联，两张红纸上面，用漂亮书法写上吉祥平安的文字，像"百岁人歌长寿酒，万年花舞太平春"等一类祝词，贴在大门上，大大增加了节日喜气洋洋的气氛。最早，人们把春联叫桃符，宋代文学家王安石的诗所说的"千门万户瞳瞳日，总把新桃换旧符"，就是这个意思。唐宋以后，人们开始用红纸写春联来代替桃木板，但名字仍旧叫桃符。到了明代，春联的叫法才确定下来，直到今天，人们在春节挂春联的习俗依旧十分红火。除

茶联书法作品

63

了春联外，在平时，人们走到任何地方也都能看到对联，商店的对联一般是"生意兴隆通四海，财源茂盛达三江"，酒楼的对联往往是"醉里乾坤大，壶中日月长"。孩子念书的学堂更加要挂对联了，有一副对联十分精彩：

风声、雨声、读书声，声声入耳　　家事、国事、天下事，事事关心

这里前面一句的风声、雨声，意义双关，是说国家危难，所以后面才接一句关心国家大事的话，孩子们坐在课堂里读书，心里不忘国家的内忧外患，所以这副对联不但文字很工整，同时它的内容也很深刻。

今天许多人爱好旅游，人们无论走到哪里，皇宫殿堂、庙宇佛殿、风景区的楼台亭榭、古村落的民居园林等，到处都有对联，例如一所庙宇，每进佛殿的殿内殿外，柱子上都挂满对联，蔚为大观，对联内容一般是"千古英雄浪淘尽，天下名山僧占多"等。民居的厅堂，对联内容一般都是一些诗礼传家的古训或人生箴言，像"退一步天高地阔，让三分心和气平"等。园林亭榭的对联往往是"苍松翠竹真佳客，明月清风是故人"等。山东济南的大名湖有一副对联很有名："四面荷花三面柳，一城山色半城湖。"文字优美，描写景色很有特点，游人们在欣赏了美丽的湖光山色之余，发现这副对联正好抒发了他们对大自然的赞叹心情。

说到这里，不知道人们有没有注意到一个现象，就是：中国的对联、书法、建筑，这三者是三位一体的，它们同时依存，相互映衬。没有对联，书法就缺乏表现内容，没有书法，对联就失去展示手段，同时又有对联又有书法，它们才可以挂起来展示。同样，没有建筑物，对联就无处挂靠，没有对联，建筑物就失去文化的光彩。对联、书法和建筑，都是中国的重要文化，如果缺少其中一样，其他两样都要显得跛脚，说得严重一点，它们甚至不成其为中国文化了。

对联趣谈

在民间，还有大量关于对联的有趣的故事广为流传。读书人的休闲消遣，除了琴棋书画以外，聚在一起就做"续对联"游戏，就是先有一个出上联，大家来对下联，看谁对得快、对得好。有时候，一个人遇到另一个人，要测试对方的学问，也往往说一句上联，看对方能不能对出下联，这样的民间故事太多太多。有一个故事说，在一个县里，邻近的甲乙两个村子，各有一个秀才，他们互相仰慕。有一天，他

们正好在两个村子的路当中相遇，在说了一些客套话之后，甲秀才就想试试对方的真本事，他根据眼前即景，说了上句"石山岩上古木枯，此木是柴"，这句话的特点是拼字游戏，山石两字加起来是岩字，古木加起来是枯，此木加起来是柴。乙秀才想了一会，一时想不出下句，为了保全面子，他谎称突然肚子痛，借口脱身，溜回家去，进了家门，看到他的妻子正好坐在帐子里给新生婴儿喂奶，他突然受到启发，立刻回身，追上甲秀才，对他说了"长巾帐里女子好，少女更妙"的下联，这里长巾加起来是帐，女子加起来是好，少女加起来是妙，甲秀才听了，连连说，对得工整、对得巧妙，佩服佩服。不过，巧妙的对联也难免有互相抄袭现象，像这个故事里的一句"此木为柴"，还有另外一个版本，是：

行书七言联

　　此木为柴，山山出　　　　因火成烟，夕夕多

这一副拼字对联除了此木加起来是柴外，山山两字加起来是出，因火两字加起来是烟，夕夕两字加起来是多，也算得上是一副十分精彩和有特点的对联。

另外有一个苏小妹难新郎的故事也很有名。苏小妹是大文豪苏东坡的妹妹，是一个才女，她的丈夫秦观，在北宋也是个出类拔萃的词人，在结婚那天，苏小妹先在新房里，当秦观送走客人后要进新房时，却被侍女拦在门外，说必须对出一句对联后才能入洞房，秦观想，续对联吗，还不容易？他看上联是"闭门推出窗前月"，想了一会，竟越想越觉得难对，这里有三个名词，要用动作连起来。半个小时过去了，还仍然没有头绪。这时候，苏东坡看外面月色好，来到花园里散步，突然看到远处新郎被关在门外，口里念念有词，一面还用手做着关窗子的动作，就知道是怎么回事了，他

65

从地上捡起一个石块，往池里一丢，那边秦观听到"扑通"一声，脑子里立刻就有下联了，下联是"投石冲开水底天"。对联对成功了，新郎可以欢欢喜喜进洞房了。

总之，千百年来文人们不知道在对联上花了多少精力，才留给后人这一份大众化的喜闻乐见的文化遗产。

Chapter 7
Antithetical Couplets

Chinese Letters And Couplets

Chinese letters were developed from pictographic marks, with each letter pronouncing one syllable. The pictographic letters must result in producing a special writing form: antithetical couplets, that is, two sentences with same number of letters, and every matched letters with matched meanings, for instance:

The upper: Two yellow orioles chirp on green willow.

The lower: One-line white egrets fly to blue sky.

The matched letters in the two sentences above, number matches number, birds match birds, verb matches verb, color matches color, and noun matches noun.

The antithetical couplets writing form appeared as early as in the Spring & Autumn Period (770—476 BC). In South & North Dynasties Period (AD420—581) , the writing of antithetical form went prevailing in every kinds of literary articles, and the tendency became so overwhelming, that people even regarded the non-antithetical works were coarse and inferior ones.

Classical Poetry And Couplets

Chinese classical poetry thrived in Tang Dynasty (AD618—907). Tang Poetry has been known as a bright pearl of human's heritage, and it had brought about great influence to Chinese literature. Tang poetry, especially the metrical-patterned poetry had some fixed rules (see chapter 5), and one of the rules was that, in a 8-line poem, four lines must be antitheses, that is, the third

A pavilion with couplets

and fourth lines must be couplets, and the fifth and sixth lines must also be couplets. In the forms of ci-poetry in Song Dynasty (AD960—1279), there were also many rules to fix some lines to be antitheses. People love many well-known antithetical couplets in Tang poetry and Song ci-poetry, because they were so excellent, ingenious, natural and fascinating. People believed that the poets might catch an occasional inspiration to pick up these superb and excellent couplets, but sometimes their works were really time-consuming, they racked their brains forgetting food and sleep for several days and even months for searching a word. Yan Shu, a great ci-poet in Song, had composed a famous couplets:

The upper line: Irretrievable flowers   fall   off

The lower line: Familiar   swallows return back

(The couplets had been translated as: Flowers fall, do what one way; Swallows return, no strangers they)

There was an interesting story about how Yan Shu composed this couplets: It is said, he initially got the second line "familiar swallows return back", and was stuck when trying to continue the first line. He wrote the line on a piece of paper, pinning it up on the wall in his study room, and pondering it over every now and then. Three months passed, and he still had yet made it done. One day, a friend called his house, and saw the paper, who thought for a moment and said: How about "Irretrievable flowers fall off"? Yan, at the hearing of the line, delighted beyond his expectations, and he then afterward finished his prestigious classical ci-poem *Wan Qi Sha* (a ci-poem brand).

In Chinese literature, poetry and couplets were two kinds of literary forms, and they were mutually dependent and mutually helping forward. Couplets made poetry more peculiar magnificent, and vice versa, poetry made couplets more refined and valuable, and enjoy much more popularity.

Couplets Seen Everywhere

Couplets could also be seen everywhere in Chinese society.

Couplets were the indispensable decorations on festival holidays. During the Spring Festival, all the families would decorate their houses with "Spring Couplets", using red papers, brushing fine calligraphy on the words of good omens and best wishes, hanging on their walls or doors, that created special cheerful atmosphere on holidays.

At ordinary times, people also hung a variety of couplets in their houses, offices, workshops, stores and schools, aiming at their business could get good lucks. A popular couplets for businessmen reading as:

The upper sentence: Trades upsurge going   to   four   seas

The lower sentence: Wealth won   coming from three rivers

A couplets usually be hung on schools, read as:

The upper: Wind sound, rain sound, chanting-book sound, every sound come into ears

The lower: Family affair, nation affair, world affair, all affairs linger in minds

In old China, the nation was crises-riddled, so, the words "wind sound and rain sound" also inferred the sufferings of the nation and people.

Now, more and more people like to make a trip during holidays. When visiting Buddhist temples, historical ruins, old residences and gardens, pavilions in scenic mountains and rivers, they could inevitably meet one thing at all tourist resorts, it is antithetical couplets. Couplets in temples usually deal with extolling phrases to Buddha's magic arts, couplets in old residences usually deal with family mottoes, while couplets in pavilions in scenic places usually deal with praising natural beauty and extending joyful feelings. For instance, a couplets in a pavilion at scenic Da Min Lake in Ji'nan, capital city of Shandong Province, read:

The upper: Four causeways gather lotus-flowers, three causeways gather willows:

Antithetical Couplets

The lower: All city encircled mountains, half city encircled lake

People after visiting and enjoying the lake's beautiful scenery, find the couplets just speaking out their feelings of admiration and appreciation.

In addition, composing couplets had been commonly used as a kind of "word play"

69

for intellectuals. When friends gathered together, they would begin playing the game. They at first had an upper sentence, then competed who would make the lower sentence earlier and better. There were actually a lot of interesting stories of the kind circulating among people long and wide.

Antithetical couplets is an important part of Chinese culture, integrating with calligraphy, hanging on halls, pavilions and all sorts of architectures, making Chinese architectures rich in special characteristics of beauty and glamour.

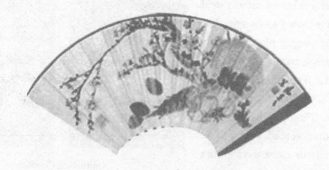

早期文学中寓言蔚为大观

寓言一般有一个故事，少的只有一段情节，讲的是简单易懂的事，但里面包含着深刻的道理或哲理，话中有话，以此喻彼，所以叫寓言。中国古典文学中寓言丰富多彩，像一座珍贵宝库，所以应该把它称为寓言文学，可以这样说，寓言文学的发达，也是中国文学中一个重要现象。

在前面第一篇里已经介绍了百家争鸣年代，春秋战国出现一批思想家著书立说，许多人为了阐述自己的理论，或驳斥别人的观点，往往在自己著作里使用寓言这个武器，其中孟子就是一个写寓言的好手。人们在《孟子》一书里看到许多精彩寓言，像"拔苗助长"的故事，可能人人都知道，所以这里就不说了，可惜今天还有不少做家长的仍在做着拔苗助长的事情。孟子有的寓言，没有完整的故事，却也很有意思，有一次，他举一个例子婉转批评一个诸侯王看不到老百姓疾苦，说："有一个人的眼睛可以看到秋天里一根很细的毫毛（秋毫之末），但是看不到一车子柴禾（不见舆薪），你能够相信吗？"后来"明察秋毫"成了成语。在孟子寓言里，挖苦人最厉害的是"齐人有一妻一妾"的

传说中的盘古

故事：有一个齐（山东）人，家中有一妻一妾（古代读书人可以有两个老婆），这个人每天傍晚回家总是摆出酒足饭饱的样子，向老婆们吹牛，今天又是哪个当官的请他吃饭了，宴席如何丰盛等。时间长了，两个老婆怀疑起来，他既然和这么多高官交际，为什么没有人上门来呢。于是有一天，等他出门，两个女人就偷偷跟在后面，只看到他走到一处坟地，那里有一家人在上坟，摆着酒菜供品，他就走过去现出一副可怜相，等人家上完坟，他低头哈腰开始乞讨。两个女人恍然明白，先回家了。到了傍晚，这个喝足吃饱的人回来了，他刚要开口吹牛，两个老婆立刻戳穿了他。这个寓言对那些吹牛人的丑态，刻画得真是入木三分。

庄子也特别擅长写寓言，也许用寓言来解释奥妙的道家观点更为传神，庄子在他的《庄子》一书里写了大量寓言，如在开头一篇"逍遥游"里，写了海里的鲲鱼和大鹏鸟，说鲲鱼长"不知有几千里也"，变为大鹏，大鹏鸟展翅把天遮住，冲天直上三万里，气象极为壮观，这无疑是在说道的境界。一篇"逍遥游"里连续出现了"越俎代庖"、"五石之瓢"、"不材之木"、"庄周梦蝶"、"庖丁解牛"和"螳臂挡车"这么许多寓言。这里说一个《庄子》里有名的"蜗角之争"的寓言：魏国决定出兵征伐宋国，大家劝阻魏王，他都不听。后来庄子去见魏王，给他讲了一个故事，说是有一只蜗牛，头上左边角上有一个国家，名叫触国，右边角上有一个国家，名叫蛮国，两个国家不断打仗争夺土地，死了数十万人，后来一方胜利了，国王趾高气扬，洋洋自得。庄子讲故事的时候，显然是用了十分鄙薄的口气，因为从道的观点看，宇宙无边，时间无极，现在两个国家打仗争土地是毫无意义的，就像蜗牛的两个角莫名其妙地争起来一样。听了这个故事后，魏王果然打消了出兵的念头。

除了孟、庄之外，战国的其他诸子也有写寓言的习惯，像列子的"愚公移山"和"杞人忧天"等，恐怕大家已经听过，现在只说一下韩非的"守株待兔"的寓言，这个故事也不详细说了，只指出一点，它的矛头像是针对儒家，意思是，过去尧舜曾经用仁义治理国家，儒家守着过去的教条，到今天是行不通的。此外，在当时许多无名史学家所写的史书里，同样也有很多寓言，如"螳螂捕蝉，黄雀在后"、"蚌鹬相争，渔翁得利"等，这里有一个"淮橘为枳"的故事比较有趣：齐国宰相晏婴有一次出使到楚国去，楚王存心要羞辱他，安排和他谈话的时候，几个士兵押着一个犯人从堂下走过，楚王故意叫住他们，问是什么犯人，回答说，是一个来自齐国的抢劫犯。楚王回过头问晏婴，你们齐国很多人都抢劫吗？晏婴说，淮南的橘子是甜的，把橘树移到淮北，它变成枳就苦了。我们齐国人本来是好的，到了楚国就变坏了。晏婴是中国第一个高明的外交家，楚王碰到他只能自讨没趣。这个寓言也有深刻哲理：一个人近朱者赤，近墨者黑，环境对人的影响是很大的。

春秋战国时期的寓言成就，肯定要对后世的寓言产生巨大影响，这里只能提一些最著名的例子。像唐代柳宗元写的寓言小品《三戒》，里面有个"黔驴技穷"的故事，说贵州本来没有驴，有人好玩把一头驴运过去，放养在山脚下，小老虎第一次看到这样的庞然大物，吓得不得了。后来经过来来回回观察试探，弄清楚驴没有本事，就把它咬死吃了。唐代白居易也写了许多寓言诗，其中"梁燕歌"为人们所熟悉，说两只燕子从筑巢到下蛋孵出四只小燕子，辛勤一个多月喂大小燕子，小燕子长大，一个早晨都随风四散飞走。两只老燕子只好伤心地守着空巢，等着它不归的子女。现在社会上出现许多膝下空虚的老人，他们有了一个名字叫"空巢老人"，形象比喻就来自白居易的这首寓言诗。

寓言和成语

寓言和成语是两个概念的东西。中国的成语体系也非常庞大发达，成语宝库内容之丰富，色彩之斑斓，是世界上其他语言所难及。成语运用在写文章中，可以帮助表达思想，增加笔墨光彩，用在人们日常交谈中，可以显得一个人谈吐优雅，语言生动。中国的成语一般都有一个典故，就是有一个来历或根据，这个现象也是独一无二的。成语典故或故事来源很广，首先是来自寓言。上面介绍了丰富多彩的寓言，可以看到，几乎每个寓言后来都转化成了一个成语，所以，寓言和成语不是同一个东西，但它们之间又有着密切的联系。

成语典故的另一个主要来源，就是历史故事。历史故事都是由历代文人或史学家记载下来的，里面的精华和警句就转化成为成语，所以这里也有文史学家的功劳。因为中国历史悠久，这类成语数量实在太多，这里举例不免顾此失彼，只好挂一漏万。例如"破釜沉舟"这个成语，表示一种丢掉一切生的希望、拼死向前的决心，它的来源是楚霸王项羽起兵攻打秦朝军队的故事。公元前207年，项羽带领部队渡漳河与秦军决战，渡河前，他下令烧掉营帐，砸掉饭锅，渡河后，又把渡船凿沉，到巨鹿和秦兵对阵时，楚国战士杀声震天，无不以一当十，击溃秦军主力。再举成语"桃李满天下"的故事：唐朝初期有个著名的贤能宰相狄仁杰，他非常重视发现和培养人才，先后向皇帝推荐了数十个优秀官员，后来他们都担当起国家重任，许多人散布在全国各地当地方官。当时有人对狄仁杰说，你这么多门生在各地当官，真可说是"桃李满天下"了。

除了历史故事形成的成语以外，还有一类成语直接来自文学家和诗人的作品，由于这些文字生动别致，寓意深刻，得到人们的喜爱和共鸣，就流传成为成语。这类成语的数量也非常多，举例也很困难，如晚唐有位诗人有一首题为《贫女》的诗，最后

常娥奔月

两句是："苦难年年压针线，为他人做嫁衣裳"，形容一个美丽的贫穷家女孩，为生活所迫，年年为别人家姑娘做出嫁的衣服，意思含蓄凄婉。诗人在这里是由怜贫女而自怜，后来"为他人做嫁衣裳"或"为人作嫁"成了一句著名的成语。苏轼有两句诗"相逢不用忙归去，明日黄花蝶也愁"，据记载，他在徐州做官时，有个朋友来看他，又要匆匆回去，当时正是赏菊日子，他就写诗挽留朋友不要走，说到明天菊花黄了，连蝴蝶也会发愁的。后来"明日黄花"成了成语。现在不少人把这句成语错说为"昨日黄花"，而且以讹传讹，应该纠正过来。后来，人们继续从文学作品里选用成语，如由《水浒》出现了成语"逼上梁山"，由《红楼梦》出现了成语"机关算尽太聪明"、"假作真时真亦假"等等。

还有一种谚语，和成语差不多，两者有何区别，人们说法也不尽一样。一般说，谚语更接近老百姓的日常生活，有农谚"瑞雪丰收年"和时谚"白露不露身"等等。许多谚语明显很通俗，像"狗急跳墙"、"狗拿耗子"、"狗眼看人低"、"狗咬吕洞宾"、"狗改不了吃屎"等，因为狗和人很接近，所以在这些语言中狗成了主角。谚语里还有关于保健的"笑一笑，十年少"，关于生活的"吃得苦中苦，方为人上人"以及"害人之心不可有，防人之心不可无"等等，不一而足。

寓言和神话

中国的寓言很发达，但神话文学却相对薄弱，尤其和古希腊辉煌的神话故事比起来，较为逊色。神话本来是上古人类对神秘宇宙的理解和想象，中国到四千年前的商代才出现文字，关于这以前的史前社会，只留下一些传说故事，一般都带有神话色彩。譬如传说中的三皇五帝时期，实际上他们都是原始部落领袖。黄帝无疑是一个领头的，在前面关于四大发明的一篇里已有他的介绍。炎帝名列其次，他又名神农氏，传说他教老百姓耕种农作物，自己还尝百草，发明用草药治病。中国人怀念黄帝和炎帝的恩泽，所以把自己叫做炎黄子孙。传说中另外还有一个有巢氏，他教老百姓在树上筑巢而居，结束了住岩洞生活。有一个伏羲氏，他教老百姓捕鱼和饲养家禽家畜。还有一个燧人氏，他教老百姓钻木取火，有了火，原始人由吃生食转为吃熟食，在文明上前进了一大步。所有这些人物虽然带有神话色彩，但大体接近实际生活，他们基本上被描写为人，而没有被描写成神。

但中国也有一些绝对称得上是神话的故事，他们出现在汉代道家人所编写的《山海经》和《淮南子》等书里，里面著名的故事，也就是像"盘古氏开天劈地"、"女娲补天"、"后羿射日"、"共工触山"等少数几个。"女娲补天"说的是：当时天漏，女娲在大荒山炼了三万六千块五彩石，各有二十四丈见方，把天空补得完整无缺。她还砍了一只大海龟的四只脚，把天空支撑起来。"共工触山"说的是：共工和黄帝的儿子争夺天下失败，他气愤地把头撞到不周山上，造成天崩地裂。天向西北斜了，所以太阳月亮都往西边走，地向东南坍了，所以河水都往东边流。神

伏羲与女娲

75

话故事荒诞不经，但它们色彩浪漫，想象奇特，人物也很有性格和感情，所以几千年来也为人们津津乐道，成为经典流传下来。

一直到了明代，神话文学有了起色。当时小说作为新的文学形式兴起，出现了两部影响很大的长篇小说《西游记》和《封神榜》。《西游记》在前面的文学篇里已经详细介绍，这里简单说一下《封神榜》：小说以周武王起兵征伐纣王（公元前1100年前后）为背景，两方对阵的都是道教两派之间的神仙和得道的精灵，他们双方都使用超人的法术和魔力，在斗争最激烈的时候，道教的始祖老子（被尊为太上老君）也不得不卷入到冲突中来。《封神榜》是一部深受人们欢迎的小说，许多故事在民间广泛流传，里面许多角色，后来都成了天兵天将，有的则成了和人们生活休戚相关的各种守护神。

Chapter 8
Fable

Fable in Early Philosophers' Works

A fable usually connoted a deep philosophical concept through telling a simple and plain story. Fable-writing showed up in China as early as the Spring & Autumn Period (770—476 BC) when many early philosophers and scholars wrote their books to reveal and propagate their ideas and doctrines, making the fable writing reach its peak. (See chapter 1) For the sake of explaining their philosophical theories and refuting others' arguments, they always wrote fables as their weapon, and the fable, therefore, became an important part of Chinese literature.

Among the scholars, Mengcius was a good hand at writing fables, and his fable named *Helping shoots grow by pulling them upward* sounded so popular through Chinese history. The story went: A farmer once did a-day-long backbreaking labor in his farm and returned home late in evening, and said: "I'm dead beating today, I've helped the shoots grow". His wife rushed to the scene, and to her great sorrow, to find that all of the shoots were dead.

Zhuangzi was also skillful for writing fables, and many of his fables had been adapted

King Huangdi's troop fight with the enemy

A fable: *Bookworm Dongguo of the wolf*

into popular idioms. One of his fable story named *Battle between snail antennas* was really interesting: In the Warring States Period, once the emperor of Chu State made his decision to launch a war against Song State. And Zhuangzi, at hearing the news, went to Chu State and called on the emperor trying to stop him by telling a fable: There were two countries occupied two antennas of a snail respectively. One occupied left antenna named Cu, and the other occupied right antenna named Man. The two countries fought each other for tens of years, causing hundreds of thousands of deaths. Finally Cu won the victory, and its emperor became very swollen and arrogant. Zhuangzi was a Toaist, and in Toaist's eye, the universe was boundless, and time was endless, so he told the story to the emperor inferring that it was pointless for scrambling any worldly trivial things. Chu emperor finally stopped launching the war.

In the meantime, many other scholars did the same, writing many famous fables as *A foolish old man who removed mountains* and *Qi-state people agitated about sky collapsing*. A scholar by name of Han Fei wrote a popular fable *Standing by a tree waiting for more hares*. The story described: Once a farmer came across a hare running to and dashing against a tree. After he got the died hare, he waited by the tree hoping he could pick more hares. The fable seemed to be a critique targeting the "benevolence policy" of Confucius doctrine. Han held, though ancient emperors had achieved in managing their country by carrying out "benevolence policy", but the time was changed, the policy couldn't help the country up to anything good today.

Fable heritage in the Spring & Autumn Period must give great impact to literature in following dynasties. In Tang Dynasty, a great man of letters Liu Zongyuan had written his popular fable essays *Three Warns*. Great poet Bai Juyi had composed many popular fable poems, among which the best renowned one named *Swallows on Roof Beam* telling a story: Two swallows made a nest on a roof beam and gave birth to four babies. The couple, through one month of hard working, brought them up. But, when the four young swallows learned flying skills, all of them had flied high and far, and then gone with the wind, left two old birds behind in the empty nest. In recent years, China have seen quite a few solitary old people who won a special given name as "empty nest old people", because their children have gone with the wind, to somewhere cities or even abroad.

In fact, the splendid view of fables written by early scholars and following generations of men of letters could be regarded as a "fable literature" as well as a characteristic feature of Chinese literature tradition.

Fable And Idiom

Idiom was also a great Chinese literature treasure house. The abundance and variety of idioms made Chinese literature extraordinary beautiful and magnificent. Chinese idiom usually had an allusion, i.e., they were borrowed from historical stories or quoted from literary works, such as fables, works of great historians, essays and poems of men of letters and poets. There were some great historians in Han Dynasty whose works were admired to have great literary significance, and many works have been quoted as popular idioms. For instance, the idiom "Destroying cooking utensils and ferry boats" was borrowed from a famous historical story of "General Xiang Yu of Chu State attacking Qin troops". In 200 BC, people's armed uprisings broke out to overthrow cruel Qin Dynasty, and Xiang Yu was the most powerful among the rebels. In the eve of decisive battle, Xiang ordered to destroy all his troops' cookers and ferry boats, made his soldiers be exposed to the condition of "victory or death". As a result, the soldiers on battlefield all fought tooth and nail, and finally annihilated enemy's elite troops. The historical stories of the kind made up a large part of the idioms.

Idioms coming from poems and assays in various dynasties also got a considerable share of them. The idiom "Making wedding clothes for other girls" was quoted from a poem in late Tang Dynasty, featuring a young pretty and clever girl born into a poor family sewed marriage clothes year by year for the neighboring rich girls.

Additionally, novels in Ming and Qing (1368—1911) dynasties also produced some popular idioms, such as the idiom "Forced to go Liangsgan to be outlaws" was quoted from the novel *Outlaws in Marshland*, meaning government oppressions forced people's rebellion. Another idiom quoted from *Dream of Red Mansion*, saying "Truth to be lie, if once lie to be truth".

Fable And Mythology

Comparing to the abundant and prosperous view of idiom, Chinese mythology seemed rather outshone and pale. There were some legends about the pristine "Three Kings and Five Emperors" era, among them, the stories about Emperor Huangdi and Emperor Yandi were most popular and influential, and Chinese people were always regarded themselves as "descendants of Huangdi and Yandi". Legends also alleged that

Youcaosi taught people to build house on trees, Suirensi taught people to acquire fire, Fuxisi taught people to raise livestock. But these legendary figures were all described as human beings rather than immortals or gods.

But China did have some real myth stories appeared in two books named *Shanhaijing* (literally meaning mountain and sea classics), and *Huainanzi* (literally meaning a scholar in south of Huai River), written by some Taoists in Han Dynasty (around 100 BC). There were dozens of most popular myth stories in the books. It was until Ming Dynasty (around 1300 AD) , there came forth two great myth novels, one was *A Trip to West* (see chapter 6), the other was *Fengshenbang* (literally offering god titles). The latter told the stories set in 1100 BC, when Emperor Wuwang, the founder king of Zhou Dynasty, attacked and perished Shang Dynasty. The duelists were all Taoist disciples and animal demons, and most of them afterwards became household names of people's beloved patron gods and legendary heroes.

宗 教

第九篇

儒 教

　　我国早有"三教九流"的说法，三教指儒、释（佛教）、道，九流指百家争鸣中几个主要派别。三教儒为首，可是，儒可不可称为教，历史上也有争议。因为宗教主要有三个特点，一是出世，说人世之外存在另一世界；二是有个超人的至高无上的神支配一切；第三还要有一个团体组织，而这三样儒家都不具备。相反，孔子不承认超人力量，他从来不说"怪力乱神"一类事，声称对死后的事，他也不知道（不知生，焉知死）。可是，儒家学说在中国的影响实在太大，自汉代儒家学说被确立为官方思想以来，这个学说统治了社会两千多年，小孩子一上学，就读儒家的书，全社会上上下下的政治秩序、伦理道德、人际关系等等，无不渗透着儒家教义。从这一角度讲，儒是一种宗教也可以说得通。关于孔孟学说，在前面第一篇里已有介绍，这里再补充几个要点。

　　儒家思想最基本的立脚点是"入世"，就是人要生活在这个世界之中，所以它的教义主要包括两大部分：第一是怎么做人，第二是怎么治理好国家。关于第一部分，孔孟都有大量的关于个人修身养性的教导。孔子认为，一个人要有治理国家的大志，而治国必须从提高个人修养做起，除了前面文章里已经说过的孝（对父母）、信（对朋友）、仁（爱心）以外，他还强调一个"和"字，说"和为贵"，"和"可以"小大由之"，就是说，"和"这个东西可大可小，用处很广。人们习惯把"和"字简单地理解为待人和气，不同别人争吵，其实，孔子的"和"包含"共处"的意思，这范围就大了，不同的人，不同的思想，不同的文化，海纳百川，还有人和动物共处，人和自然共处。这样看来，今天人们提出的和谐社会的目标，孔子已经有了设想的雏形了。关于怎么治理好国家，儒家也提出了一系列观点，孔子提出君王要施仁政，就是要爱民，孟子进一步提出民为贵，君为轻。清代一个文学家还总结了"礼义廉耻"的治国四字方针，说"礼义廉耻，国之四维（基础），四维不张，国乃灭亡"。这里，礼可解释为行为规范，义是正义和道德，廉是清廉俭朴，耻是不要做坏事。孔子说"知耻近乎勇"，任何一个人，如果不知耻，他就是不可救药了。不过，儒家的理论只体现了"人治"的境界，孔子非常痛恨法治，提倡完全依靠个人品性和自觉来治理国家，不讲对权力的约束，这就造成很大的偏颇。

佛　教

佛教是世界三大教（佛、基督、伊斯兰）之一，发源于天竺（印度），创建人释迦牟尼，佛教在东汉时期大约公元67年传入中国，当时的皇帝晚上梦见一个满身披着日月光的菩萨从天而降，第二天就问大臣们，这是何方神灵，有个博学者说，天竺有神，名叫佛。皇帝就欣然派了十八个人到西域（新疆一带）去请佛求经。七年后，这些人带回来三个天竺高僧，还用白马背来一些佛像和经书，皇帝下令在洛阳造一所佛庙来储存佛

白马寺

经，这个寺庙就被命名为白马寺。佛教传入中国以后，它修正了原来的教义，吸收了儒家学说内容，以适应当时环境，所以从南北朝（公元420—581年）开始，佛教就在中国流行起来，甘肃的敦煌莫高窟，在五百个岩洞里，有琳琅满目的佛像彩绘壁画，山西的云冈石窟，河南的龙门石窟，里面刻着姿态各异的佛像，这许多作品都是在那个时期创作的。唐代诗人杜牧的诗句"南朝四百八十寺，多少楼台烟雨中"，说明这时南京周围也有数不清的寺庙了。

玉佛坐像

在中国佛教史上还有两件事值得一提。一是唐僧取经。经过南北朝长期分裂，佛门派别众多，佛经也传得很乱，于是，唐代早期有一个名叫陈玄奘的和尚，决心到天竺去取"真经"，他大概在公元630年前后出发，经过十七年时间，终于取回了六百多部梵文（印度古文）佛经。他的事迹本身就是一个传奇，所以在明代出现了以唐僧取经为主线的神话小说《西游记》。另外一件事也发生在唐代，就是鉴真和尚东渡日本。唐代经济文化高度发达，日本派十二批学者和僧人，先后到中国来学习，鉴真应他们邀请到日本去，但连续渡海五次都失败了，这时鉴真又患了眼病，不久失明，他坚韧不拔，于公元742年再次东渡，终于成功到达日本。日本在奈良建了一座宏伟寺庙，鉴真主持讲经，成了日本佛宗的始祖。

佛教教义惩恶劝善，要求老百姓慈悲为怀，不杀生，不做坏事，多做好事。说人死后，灵魂进入转世轮回，一个人活着时表现好，灵魂就可以投胎到富贵人家，如果表现很坏，就被打入地狱，甚至变成一条狗。佛教还认为人的一生，一切祸福都有命中注定的因果，但如果做了很多的好事或坏事，他的命运，包括寿命都可以改变，等等。

道 教

道家和道教是两个不同概念，道家是一个学派，而道教是一种宗教。中国古时候

道教推崇的神

一直有巫师和方士一类人在民间活动，在佛教传入以后，他们得到启发应该组织起来，于是在东汉中期，大概在一千八百多年前，由一个名为张道陵的人，尊老子为始祖，奉老子的《道德经》为经典，创建了道教。老子和庄子学说强调出世，道教进一步描绘天上和海外存在的仙境，居住着各路神仙。和佛教的追求来世不同，道教认为一个凡人经过修炼，就可以成仙，达到长生不老。在道教历史中，也有两个人特别值得一提。一个是晋代的葛洪，他把儒家的忠孝信义等思想引进道教，说多做善事和为国家立功也可以成仙。另外，他还精通医术，发明"炼丹"。丹可治病，吃了可以延年益寿。长生不老对人们总是有巨大吸引力的，以后有不少皇帝热衷于炼丹求仙，但有的吃了丹后造成重金属中毒。另一个人是宋代的张三丰，他创建了有特色的道家功夫，因为他住在武当山，所以叫武当派功夫，他同时还发明了太极拳，人们经常打太极可以保健强身。到今天，太极拳越来越受到中老年人的欢迎，而且声名远播海外。

在唐代，道教和佛教之间的斗争非常激烈，主要是要得到皇帝的信任。当时，某个皇帝信佛，就下令全国大建佛庙，大拆道观，等儿子登位做皇帝，他信道教，就下令大建道观，大拆佛庙，拆拆建建，劳民伤财。在社会上，两大教派也是长期争夺信徒，佛教劝人为善，道教劝人成仙，此外，道士还为老百姓驱鬼治病，因为过去人们相信，所有疾病都是由恶鬼作祟引起，把鬼赶走，病就好了。两教不断较量的结果是，到目前，佛庙多了，道观少了，信佛的人多起来，道教的影响逐渐缩小了。

儒释道的文化和社会影响

由于在中国两千多年封建社会里，儒家学说一直占统治地位，儒家思想扎根在人

四大天王

们头脑中，影响无处不在，儒家思想对中国文化影响是如此之大，甚至可以说，没有儒家思想，中国文化就不成其为中国文化。

不过，儒释道三教经过两千年长期共存，已经互相渗透，水乳交融。宋代的几位儒家在理论上把佛和道的精神融进儒学，创造了新的"理学"，所以有人说中国文化实际上是一体两翼，儒是主体，佛和道是两翼。儒释道对中国文化和社会的影响，大体表现在下面几个方面：第一，儒和道的思想渗透在所有早期文学和史学经典里，历代知识分子都是读这些书长大，所以数千年来知识分子的思想意识非儒即道，没有一

85

个例外。第二，节日、民风、民俗是表现民族文化的第一个窗口，例如春节祭天地祖宗，挂春联放鞭炮以及合家团圆等，都是属于儒家传统，清明扫墓和中秋团聚也来自儒家渊源，而七夕的牛郎织女相会和重阳的登高故事，都具有道教色彩。第三，表现在人们日常生活习俗上，生老病死，婚庆丧葬，儒家一直提倡勤劳节俭，不过，今天有些情况却在走向反面，许多人钱并不多，但炫富、攀比、浪费、暴殄天物等行为愈演愈烈，炫富可能是中国人的一种民族劣性。第四，中国人的性格一般都显得文静敦厚，习惯忍耐，知足常乐，多一事不如少一事，等等，这些都说不清是属于儒释道的哪一个教了，就像许多人进了一个庙，不管看到什么神仙和佛像，都会跪下磕头一样。

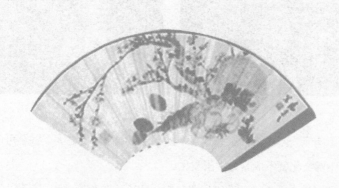

Chapter 9

Religions

Ru (Confucius) Religion

There was a Chinese idiom "Three religions and nine schools". Three religions were Ru Religion, Buddhism and Taoism, and nine schools referred some major academic schools in the Spring & Autumn Period (770 — 476 BC). Ru was the most important religion among the three, because it had become an official ideology guideline dominating the country for thousands of years. In old time, all school textbooks were Confucius' teachings, Confucius doctrine infiltrated all fields of society: political system, ethic and moral concepts, and people's life style. Confucius philosophy was a philosophy of "entering into world" (Taoism was escaping away from world), so, it contained mainly two parts: Firstly, how intellectuals could cultivate themselves, the second, how they could manage country affairs. (Please see detailed explanations in chapter 1) In addition, Confucius put emphasis on developing "He", a word could be interpreted as peace, harmony and friendship. One of Confucius students once praised highly to the word "He" as a precious concept, as it could apply to settle a variety of problems big or small. "He" also put inclusion of creating a co-existence and harmonious relations among people with different ideological and cultural backgrounds, even compatible relations between human and other living beings, between human and nature.

But Confucius, in his doctrine, only stood for "ruling by man" instead of "ruling by law". He hated the Law School's theory and practice, criticizing it "cruel politics" "as brutal as tiger". As a result, he only believed people's self-cultivation and their own moral integrity, and eliminated the necessity of restriction and supervision of political power, that made his doctrine seem stereotyped and defective.

Buddhism

Buddhism was one of the most important three religions in the world (Buddhism, Christianity, Islam). Buddhism spread in China in Late Han Dynasty (around 67 AD). The emperor, after once dreamed to meet a Buddha, assigned envoys to India, and seven

Buddha sculpture in Dunhuang

years later accepted three Indian monks and a batch of Buddhist sutras carried by a white horse. The emperor ordered to build a temple, named White Horse Temple in Luoyang City, Henan Province to collect the sutras. (The White Horse Temple is now still existed and to be a hot tourist spot) Buddhism began to develop during the South & North Dynasties Period (420—581), and people could as yet appreciate early Buddhist arts attractions created during the Period: beautiful frescoes in Dunhuang, Gansu Province, excellent stone sculptures of Buddha in Yungang Grotto in Shanxi Province, and Longmen Grotto in Henan Province. Buddhist doctrine mainly wanted to advise people to be kind-hearted and avoid doing evil things. People do anything good or evil in present life, he must get retribution in his next life. There were two important events in Chinese Buddhism history. One was "Tang monk tripped to West Heaven to acquire Buddhism sutras". In early Tang Dynasty, there circulated some incorrect sutras in China, and a monk named Chen Xuanzhuang tried to go to India attempting to acquire true sutras. It took him for 17 years to bring back whole Buddhism sutras (around 640 AD). Besides, the monk had learned Indian ancient language and translated the sutras into Chinese. The monk's deed seemed as a kind of myth people unheard of, so the stories were adopted by the novelist Shi Nan'an who wrote the novel *A Trip to West* (see chapter 6). The other was "Monk Jianzhen went to Japan". At first, he endeavored six consecutive times of voyage, but all failed. By the time, Jianzhen suffered a serious eye disease and became blind, but it couldn't stop him. Finally in his seventh voyage, he went successfully across the sea, and arrived his destination. Monk Jianzhen brought Buddhism to Japan, and a variety of Chinese cultures as well. Jianzhen made him the Japanese earliest Buddhist ancestor.

Taoism

Taoism School and Taoism Religion were two different things. Taoism School was one of philosophical schools created by Laozi in the Spring & Autumn Period. (see chapter 1) Shortly after Buddhism came in, a Taoist named Zhang Daoling founded

Taoism Religion in Han Dynasty by honoring Laozi as its original ancestor. Taoism religion asserted there were celestial beings living in the Heaven, and people could also become immortals through some process of self-cultivation. The Taoist priests also treated diseases for people by catching or driving away ghosts or demons. (People in old time attributed their diseases to ghost's haunting) There were also two important figures in Taoism history, one was Ge Hong in Jin Dynasty (265—420), who initiated to make so-called "immortality pills", by putting some organic and inorganic ingredients burning in the furnace. The other was Zhang Sanfeng in Song Dynasty (960—1279) who invented Wudang Taoist kung fu (as he lived at Wudang Mountain, in north Hubei Province) as well as Tai Ji, the shadow boxing. Up-to-date, the Tai Ji has become more popular than ever to be a fitness exercise especially accepted by mid aged and elderly people.

Cultural Impacts of Three Religions

After having dominated Chinese politics, social ideology and people's lifestyle for thousands of years, Ru (Confucius) philosophy had brought about a dominating impact to Chinese culture. Chinese culture would have been something else if it happened without Ru's doctrine. But historians believed that Ru Religion, Buddhism and Taoism had later well-blended together in China, Ru was the principle part, Buddhism and Taoism were the two wings. People could see the influences of the three religions as following: 1. Ru and Taoism philosophies had infiltrated all the early literary and historical classics that had nurtured and brought up intellectuals generation by generation, so the "world outlook" of every individual intellectual had inevitably carried Ru or Taoism conceptions. 2. Chinese traditional festivals were usually the occasions fully reflecting folk cultures. The customs of family reunion, worshipping Heaven and forbears, hanging spring couplets and setting off firecrackers in the

Giant Buddha of Leshan Mountain

89

Spring Festival were the tradition of Ru, while the customs of marking the reunion of the Weaving Girl and Cowboy in the Seven-Clever Festival and climbing mountain activity in the Double-Ninth Festival were the tradition of Taoism. (see chapter 3) 3. In day-to-day life, Ru religion advised people practicing thrifty and diligent. (But in present day, some young people act as just opposite) 4. The nature and character of most Chinese people were gentle, endurable, yielding, and playing safe when facing trouble. It might be a mixed religious behavior, something like some people would kneel in front of any god they met when they entering a temple.

中国文字的起源和发展

中国史书上传统说法是仓颉造字。仓颉是史前时代黄帝的一个记事官，而现在考古发现最早的文字，是距今三千年的商代的甲骨文。甲骨文是刻在龟甲和动物骨头上的文字，出土地点是河南安阳（商代原来的都城），文字总共有三千多个。目前，专家已破译出其中约一千个，认为当时文字不论从数量、句式和表达力，都已经发展到相当高的水平。由于文字发展需要一个漫长过程，专家估计从简单符号发展到甲骨文，大约经过了一千到两千年，这时间大体符合仓颉造字的说法。那为什么没有发现商代以前的甲骨文呢？可能是在甲骨上刻字需要锋利的刀，而刀到商代才有。

中国文字最早从象形开始，像日、月、山、水等，文字要表达复杂的意思，古人采用了六种造字的方法，因为比较专业，这里不详细谈了，沿着这条路，中国字发展成为单个的方块字。因为全世界外国人都用拼音文字，他们看方块字就觉得很神秘。其实，方块字一点也不复杂，恐怕比拼音字更加容易学习和记忆。这里拿一个字来解剖一下：苗字，田上长出草头，就是苗，苗字可以引申出拔苗、苗圃、苗条、苗头等词汇，如果在苗字边上加字，边上加犬成猫

甲骨文

91

（又可引申出猫眼、猫腻、猫头鹰等），加手成描（又可引申出素描、描绘、描摹、描写等），加金成锚，加目成瞄，等等。可以说，所有的中国文字的词汇，都是这样两两配合而成的，单个方块字常用的不过约一千个，经过互相交叉结合，就千变万化，奥妙无穷了。中国字还有许多讨巧的地方，像一月到十二月、星期一到星期日，很简单，不像英语每一月每一日都有单独的一个单词。还有像哮喘、糖尿病、老年痴呆等病症，都从字面上可以看出来。所以，对中国的方块字，只要认识一千个左右，并且掌握它的规律，它还是易懂易学的。

再回来谈文字发展。甲骨文到周代中期演变成大篆，就是蝌蚪文。春秋战国时期的大部分蝌蚪文，后来都被秦始皇烧掉，所以有一个文人写了首歪诗：田间有蝌蚪，分明古篆文，只因藏水下，秦火不能焚。秦始皇灭六国建立秦朝后，为了统一文字，就创造了小篆，就是现在人们刻印章的字体。小篆体到汉代很快变化成隶书，到汉末三国时期，楷书就出现了，这里看得出毛笔发明后所起的作用。楷书就是今天人们使用的文字，到晋代已完全定型，它的代表就是王羲之的作品。到唐代宋代，草书和行书同时流行起来，行书是一种比较实用的字体。

书法艺术

书法是中国独有的一门艺术，外国文字虽然也有艺术字，但和中国书法的性质完全不同。中国书法的形成有下列几个要素：

一、中国文字一开始就有形象思维因素，随着字体变形，越来越注意每个字的形象，如篆体字的形状结构就很匀称流畅，在字体向隶书和楷书的变形中，在求得书写方便的同时，人们没有忽略字的造型美，相反，文字更有意识地向艺术靠拢。

二、使用了毛笔这样的特殊书写工具，就是说，用毛笔书写中国字可以成为书法，书法一定需要用毛笔，没有毛笔，也就没有书法（现代，在此基础上，出现了硬笔书法）。根据记载，毛笔是秦国的一个大将军蒙恬发明的，当时文字是用刀刻在竹片上，因为前方军情变化大，蒙恬为了向国王及时报告，集中大量人力日夜刻字还是来不及。当时北方战场上狼和羊很多，蒙恬就用狼毛或羊毛，用线把它们扎在一根树枝上，蘸上颜料，把字写在丝绸上，速度就快多了。不过，近几年有考古专家在考古发掘时出土一支早期毛笔，测试证明，它比蒙恬的年龄还要大一点。因为蒙恬是个名人，那支毛笔的主人无名无姓，看来为这事翻案也不必了。

三、书法还和中国知识分子的秉性和追求有关，它们成了知识分子显示自己个性和爱好，表达自己理想、趣味和精神境界的重要形式。本来文字和书写是人们的日常生活行为和人际交流的工具，如记事、写信等，它们一般是用小楷和中楷，一些名家的书信和所有的墨迹，片纸只字，光彩照人，因此都被看成是精品墨宝，后来人们写的大楷、行书、草书之类，都成了专门的书法艺术。书法家们在闲暇日、寂寥时，往往舞文弄墨，以此消遣时光，陶冶情趣，这种在不经意和完全放松状态下写成的作品，会更充分表达他们的个性和奔放的感情。可以说，世界上没有任何艺术，能够像书法那样，尽善尽

米蒂字

美地表达艺术家的内心世界，释放他们的思想感情。

这里附带说一点，唐宋以后，出现了书法和绘画结合的趋向，当时有些画家，在画好一幅画以后，请著名的诗人或书法家，在画上补写一段书法（也有的是画家自己题字的），这样绘画和书法珠联璧合，它们的艺术性就更高了。后来，人们又在绘画和书法作品上盖印章，印章也是一门独立的艺术门类，书法、绘画、印章三种艺术，在同一幅作品里互相烘托，交相辉映。后来盖印章的人越来越多，每个收藏家都要在收藏的作品中盖上自己的印章，连历代皇帝收藏的字画，上面也要盖上"御览之宝"的大印。结果现在许多历史文物珍品，上面变得印章密布，蔚为奇观。

最后来说一说怎样欣赏书法艺术。因为书法是一门特殊艺术，它只有线条，不依靠外加的任何图像和色彩，它就要挖掘线条本身的丰富多变的表现力和艺术性。譬如，有的线条刚劲，有的活泼，有的含蓄，还有的用一段飞白表现飘逸，等等，在一幅书法作品中，甚至每一个字里，都蕴藏着丰富的内涵和变化。这里说一个上面提

到的晋代书法家王羲之的故事：他有一幅代表作叫《兰亭序》，那天朋友聚会，他喝得酩酊大醉，写字时，提笔落纸如云烟，等到醒来一看，里面有几个错字，还有几个字歪斜不像样，就圈掉重写，但可以看得出，他在酒醉时候写的字个个豪迈奔放，神采奕奕，而在酒醒后改写的字，虽然工整无可挑剔，但却失去了灵性。书法还和一个人的文化修养和知识底蕴有着极大关系，例如北宋的书法四大家，他们之间的书法功力水平，应该是难分伯仲的，但经过后代书法家的反复评议，最终一致认为四大家当中，苏轼位列第一，因为苏轼学识渊博，才华横溢，智慧如浩瀚大海，这赋予他的书法一种特殊的意境，因而它的高度别人难以达到。

中 国 画

中国有"书画同源"的说法，这有几重意思：一是书法家和画家生活在同一个社会文化大环境里，他们有共同的文化和艺术理念，许多人既是书法家，也是画家。知识分子把书法和绘画同样看作是表现志趣和追求，传达个人思想感情的工具；二是写书法和画画都是用毛笔，就是说，用同一个法宝，下笔方法也有点相通，譬如，用写篆字的笔法画树干，用写草书的笔法画线条等；三是书画家们往往把诗词、书法、绘画和印章糅合在同一幅作品里，数种艺术融为一体。

中国的绘画也源远流长，几千年历史，数十个朝代，出现了数不清的优秀画家和绘画作品，可以说每个朝代都有几个画家的名字掷地有声。中国最早发现的美术作品是出土的新石器时代（距今五千到六千年）的彩陶画，有个彩陶鱼纹盆上的鱼，线条粗犷流畅，鱼眼炯炯有神，鱼嘴也勾画生动，表现了先民画师的高超技能。其他出土的彩陶画，还有蛙、鹿、花、鸟等内容。但是，从春秋战国到汉代唐代，绘画作品保留下来的就很少，原因是画家多半把画画在墙壁上，当时的佛庙壁画很多，据说像王维和吴道子这样的大师，也把画画在庙宇的墙上，但房屋坍塌了，画也随之湮灭，倒是画在墓道里的壁画，现在发现后才得以保存下来。还有就是画家把画画在丝绸上，杜甫有一首十分著名的诗，讲皇帝叫画家曹霸进宫，在丝绸上画马的故事。但是，丝绸很贵，丝绸画又很难保管，所以流传到今天的极少。人们替那个时代的画家想想，除了墙壁，确实没有可供他们发挥才能的地方，于是，在遥远的西北部，出现了一个壁画宝库，这就是闻名世界的敦煌莫高窟壁画。因为敦煌地处丝绸之路的中国的一端，是当时一个商旅重镇，驼铃叮当，境况繁华，艺术家也集中到这里来，从公元366年的晋代开始，在这里作画延续了十个朝代，莫高窟就成了世界上罕有的宏伟艺术宝库。到宋代，朝廷专门成立了翰林画院，中国画中的山水画、人物画和花鸟画已经分别形成了独立门类。

中国画还有一个总的指导思想："外师造化，内法心源"，什么意思呢？就是说外部事物只是一个依据，绘画必须通过画家的思想感情。中国画不讲究形似，而重在神似，它不像西洋画那样讲透视、视角、比例、远近、明暗等原则，而是可以不受限制地把形象任意歪曲夸张，例如把船画在山顶上、画鱼不画水等。中国画还特别强调"藏"的手法，像画一片云把山藏起来，画几棵树把水藏起来，避免给人一眼看穿。还有更离奇的例子是，唐代

郎世宁画

画家王维画的《雪里芭蕉》，芭蕉是夏季植物，怎能长在雪里？宋代画家苏轼用红笔画竹子，这看来更荒唐了，但他们在画里传达的是思想，人们还是认可它们，这些都是中国画"外师造化，内法心源"的例子。人们如不懂这个道理，在欣赏中国画的时候，就可能会迷惑不解。

中国画的主流是写意，但也有过写实的作品，代表作是北宋的《清明上河图》，作者是张择瑞，像是个宫廷画家。这是一幅长卷，高25厘米，横528厘米，内容是描写宋代京都开封（原叫汴京）的繁华景色，在画面里一共出现了550个人物，有读书人、商人、医生、商店杂工、和尚、道士、官吏、算命看手相的、妇女和孩子、船上的船工，以及在酒店喝酒的、逛街的、围在桥上看热闹的、几个人聊天的、坐轿的、骑马的，除此以外，还画了房屋三十多幢，汴河上大小船只二十多条，牛、马、驴、骆驼五十多头。画卷一头从郊区生机盎然的农田和几头小毛驴、几个人开始，逐渐推

汪士慎的画

进城区，形形色色的人越来越多，房舍越来越稠密，然后来到一座大拱桥，横跨汴河，这里就是市中心了。整个画面构图严谨，众多的人物姿势神态各异，所有细微处画笔一丝不苟。这幅画生动真实，气势宏大，视野广阔，不失为一件难得的顶级国宝。

到了元代明代，这时期的绘画精品流传到今天的就多起来了。这里要提到一个人，是明末清初的朱耷。他姓朱，是明代皇室家系的人，明亡后他出家当了和尚。在这以前，中国画大都是工笔画，就是整个画面很工整，用笔用色很精细，朱耷的贡献就是，他开创了用简单笔墨写意，也就是随意挥洒的画风，寥寥几笔，就画成功一幅画。他善画花鸟，但他画的鸟多是枯柳孤鸟、枯木孤鸟、竹石孤鸟等，找不到欢快气氛，尤其是鸟的眼睛很怪，有点朝上翻。他自己号称八大山人，八与大两字连写，又像哭字又像笑字，他大概就要在画里表现这种思想感情。

朱耷的画风和中国书法更加接近了一步，它对清代，以至近代现代的画家影响都很大，以后人们所见到的中国画及目前流行的中国画，绝大多数都是简笔的写意画了。

Chapter 10
Calligraphy And Painting

Chinese Written Letters

Chinese people called their written letters as "square letters", that originated and developed from pictographic inscriptions. Archeologists discovered inscriptions on bones and tortoise shells of Shang Dynasty (1562—1066 BC) in Anyang County, Henan Province. The inscriptions featured mainly the records on activities of paying worships to heaven, and the number of the pictographic letters reached as many as 3 thousands. Chinese written letters had experienced several major transformations during following 1,700 years, especially Han Dynasty (206 BC—220 AD) saw a significant change of written letters' form because of the invention of Chinese writing brush. As the pictographic letter itself was something like an art form, our ancestors had also laid great stress on the improvement of letters art style when transforming them. People could see there was already without any difference of letter forms between modern written letters and that written by Wang Xizhi, a great calligrapher in Jin Dynasty (265 AD—420).

Calligraphy

Chinese calligraphy is an art style genuine in Chinese nature and characteristics. The calligraphic art took the roots of three essential elements: The first, it took the root of Chinese written letter form itself (been related above). The second, it took the root of writing tool, the writing brush. Only the Chinese brush produced Chinese calligraphy, and only Chinese calligraphy made use of writing brush. It is said, Meng Tian, a military commander of Qin State in the Warring States Period (475—221 BC) was the inventor of the brush. In the battlefield, Meng was asked to offer battle reports to the emperor, though he had employed a lot of people to engrave letters on bamboos, but he still often missed deadlines. One day, he came across an idea, that he could avail animal hair to make a writing tool, as the desolated border area abounded in hares, deer and sheep. The initial brush he made was only a tree twig been bound with animal hair, but for his great joy, the brush really did a good job. And in following dynasties, people

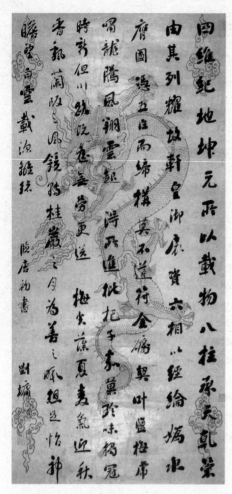

Calligraphy work

had renovated consecutively the brush and made it more and more beautiful and practical. Thirdly, Chinese calligraphy also had an important bearing on intellectuals' hobby and aspiration. At first, writing letters was a regular work for their day-to-day life, keeping memorandum for oneself or exchange messages with relatives and friends. But people found someone's brief notes of calligraphy appeared so beautiful that they would became a kind of art works. Then gradually calligraphy became an independent art style, and brushing calligraphy became a pastime or hobby for calligraphers. Especially at their leisure time, when the calligraphers wielded their brushes as a way for recreation or relaxing their temperament, the calligraphy works could always reach their exquisite and superb level because the works could fully display calligraphers' nature and sentiments of their inner mind.

In Tang and Song dynasties, calligraphy showed a tendency to integrate with painting and chop. In the beginning, some painters asked famous poets or calligraphers to add an inscription and a chop on their paintings (sometimes the painters did it by themselves), and finally the three forms of arts, painting, calligraphy and seal were integrated together.

Calligraphy, as an art form, has neither picture image nor color. When appreciating calligraphy works, people would taste the brushing lines: some strong and bold, some elegant and lively, and some rich in varieties and vividness. More, the contents of calligraphy were usually a poem, couplets, motto, or other rhythmic prose, that reflecting calligrapher's aspirations.

Traditional Painting

A Chinese saying went: There was a same source for calligraphy and painting. The word indicated three facts: The first, calligraphers and painters were all intellectuals who had the same cultural background under Confucius teachings. The second, they used the same tool, the writing brush. The third, calligraphers and painters always created their works combining calligraphy, painting and seal together.

In present time, paintings in Tang and Song dynasties are rare to be seen because the ancient artists only created their paintings on pieces of silk or on the walls of Buddhist or Taoist temples. Besides the wall and silk, there was actually no other place providing them to display their arts skills. But when the temple collapsed, their paintings would also fall into oblivion. And the silk as well, was also difficult to be preserved. The ancient paintings painted on the walls and been well-preserved up-to-date were only in Dunhuang Grottos in Gansu Province.

What Chinese traditional painting differed from western painting was that the images in Chinese painting were of fabrications. Chinese traditional painting was put stress on "display man's sentiments", rather than "display the real world". Chinese intellectuals highly admired pine, bamboo and plum, honoring them a title as "three friends in cold winter", praising them for their noble nature of withdrawal and perseverance under harsh conditions. As a result, "the three friends in cold winter" had actually become a constant subject matter for Chinese painting. Chinese painters also adhered an important criterion that the images they painted were their imagined world, i.e., they could or must transform images in accordance with their subjective willingness, in other word, the images displayed in the painting were painter's own aspirations. For example, they could paint boats above mountains, or paint fish and shrimps out of water. Chinese painters also applied a common skill of "hiding something", i.e., hiding mountains by painting clouds, hiding river by painting trees, etc. There were two typical examples of "display sentiments", one was Wang Wei's (in Tang Dynasty) *Banana And Snow*, but banana was never existed amidst snow. The other was Su Shi's (in Song Dynasty) *Red*

Chinese painting

A chop

Bamboo, but bamboo's color was always green. Though these images were absolutely unreasonable, people could still make sense and appreciate them.

At the turn of Ming and Qing dynasties (around 1650), there came forth a painter named Zhu Da whose style of painting gave a significant impact on that of later generations. Zhu was a imperial family member of Ming Dynasty, and he became a Buddhist monk after the fall of Ming Empire. Before Zhu's appearance, the painting style dominating for more than thousand years was "Gongbi style", meaning careful and neat style. Painters painted everything, a bird or a flower for example, with intensive and meticulous strokes of lines and colors. Zhu's contribution was that he initiated a new style of painting called "Jianbi style", meaning simple style. He painted everything with brief and simplified strokes by sprinkling ink and color on the paper. But the images Zhu painted were usually *Dead Tree And Solitary Bird*, *Withered Willow And Solitary Bird*, or *Stone Bamboo And Solitary Bird*, in a word, people could only see bleak and depressed feelings from his works. After Qing Dynasty, including modern time, painters were mostly inherited Zhu's brief and simplified style. Now when some people witnessed a painter made his work done by sprinkling ink and color in a few minutes, they began to doubt: Could these kind of painting finished so easily be worthy of a high price? But they didn't know how long it took for the painter been trained and practiced to get his basic arts cultivation.

戏　剧

第十一篇

中国戏剧沿革

中国戏剧最早的雏形，是史前社会原始人的表演，带各种面具，边唱边跳。一直到公元250年的三国时期，有一次，有两个书生玩文字游戏，说好谁出题难倒对方者获胜，有一人输了后恼羞成怒，违反君子动口不动手的协定，两个人打起来，结果拳头是硬道理，力气大者获胜。蜀国君主刘备把这个故事编成戏，叫人来表演。这是史书记载的第一次具有真正意义的戏剧演出。中国戏剧一开始就和文学、音乐、舞蹈结合在一起，所以也叫戏曲。到唐代，风流皇帝唐玄宗在皇宫的梨园里蓄养了七八百人的歌舞戏曲班子，他自己也常常登台演出或弹奏乐器。所以，后来人们把从事戏曲行业的人叫梨园子弟。

中国戏曲的繁荣要从元代（1260—1368）算起，由于城市的发展，出现了市民阶层和他们的文化娱乐需要，社会上纷纷建立各种演戏和说书场所。同时，元代蒙古族统治者取消了科举取士，读书人断了做官的道路，只好把注意力转到文学戏曲创作上来。元代初期，在京城北京就出现了一批名声卓著的戏剧家和他们的传世经典作品，他们奠定了中国传统戏曲的基础。元曲继承了宋词的传统，并开始出现独立的曲调，每个曲调有个曲牌名称，叫散曲，后来剧作家们在剧本里融进大量的曲调，它们文字委婉清丽，色彩斑斓，讲究韵味，兼有优美动听的曲子。由于元曲的整体文学和艺术成就极高，它成了中国文学发展的一个阶段性标志，中国文学大体上是沿着唐诗、宋词、元曲（包括戏曲和散曲）、明清小说等阶段发展过来的。

京 剧

京剧是中国的国剧，被全国人民引以为豪，海内外人士一致赞誉它是中国文化的精粹。它有深厚的文化艺术底蕴，是一门集文学、戏剧、歌唱、表演和美术为一体的综合艺术，而且两百多年来名家层出不穷，各种流派争奇斗艳，积累了丰富的表演经验和程式，以及魅力无穷的保留剧目。那么，京剧是在什么时候，又是怎样形成的呢？

清初，北京剧坛的盟主是昆剧，1780年，乾隆皇帝过八十岁生日，南方官员带了一个名叫"三庆"的安徽戏班子参加庆祝活动，大受赞赏，不久，另外三个安徽戏班子也陆续来到，形成四个安徽戏班统领北京舞台的局面，逐渐取代了昆剧，这就是京剧出现的前期。到1828年，又有一个湖北的剧团来到北京，安徽戏又把湖北戏的许多优点吸纳进来，经过兼容改进，一个新的剧种最终出现了，人们正式叫它为京剧。京剧很快在全国各大城市，尤其是上海和天津发展起来，成为全国性最大剧种，并在后来的两百多年时间里有了长足发展。

京剧的特点有哪些？它主要表现在三个方面：一是角色有统一的造型。人们看京剧第一个印象，就是角色的脸谱和化妆，它让人一眼看出角色是个什么人，是好人还是坏人。京剧中角色分四大类，就是："生、旦、净、丑。""生"意思是男人，里面又分小生（年轻人）、武生和老生；"旦"是女人，里面又分花旦、青衣（地位低的年轻女性）、老旦和刀马旦等；"净"包括的人群比较复杂，像公侯将相、忠臣奸臣、神灵魔怪等等，都属这一类；"丑"就是丑角，一般地位也比较低，表演带点滑稽和搞

京剧《玉簪记》

笑。关于四类角色的脸谱和化妆，"生"一般不画脸谱，像皇帝、读书人、文人学者，他们一般都是正面人物；"旦"也不画脸谱，但化妆很讲究，尤其是花旦，也是戏中女主角，脸部浓妆，从头到脚珠光宝气；京剧脸谱集中在"净"一类角色里，花花绿绿，争奇斗艳，所以老百姓叫他们为"花脸"。脸谱的颜色也很有讲究，红色表示忠诚，像三国戏里的关公；黑色表示勇猛，像项羽和张飞；满脸白色表示奸诈，像曹操；还有蓝色表示妖魔；黄金色表示天上神灵等。所有脸谱都是用这些颜色混合勾画出来，象征一个人的身份和个性；至于"丑"一类角色，他们毫无例外地在鼻子上抹一大块白粉，眉毛画成倒挂，以达到丑的目的。

梅兰芳京剧戏装

二是表演的程式化。程式化是中国传统戏剧表演的最大特点，总的包括唱、念、做、打四个部分。先来说唱，在大量的剧目中，唱是京剧表演的灵魂，每当剧情进入重要环节，剧中人总是通过大段的唱来抒发内心的思想感情。京剧唱段文字非常优雅抒情，像诗一样，还有韵味，曲调也美妙动听，所以唱是一个京剧演员最重要的基本功，许多名噪一时的京剧表演艺术家，都是以创新的独特的唱段自创一派，引领潮流，许多京剧的经典保留剧目，也是因为有独到的唱段魅力而长演不衰；再来说念，就是说台词，因为京剧里说话用"韵白"（白意思是说话，韵白是带韵味的说话），所以叫做"念"。念韵白用假嗓子、变节奏或夸张的语调，角色不同，念韵白的声调也不一样，譬如，"小生"说话用又尖又高的假嗓子，"净"一般嗓音宽大洪亮等。"念"也是京剧演员的一门基本功，韵白也能提高京剧的艺术境界，但因为韵白比较难懂，现在一些新编的京剧就尽量少用或不用它，而改用普通话了；还有"做"，就是表演。京剧里的表演，和一般戏剧电影里的表演也有很大不同，它规定了许多程式，譬如，戏一开始，有一个老人踱着方步上场，走到台中央在一把椅子上坐下，开始自报家门，交代自己叫什么名字，年龄多大，家里有几个人，是做官的还是做生意的，现在发生了一件什么事，等等。如果上场的是个年轻女子，她还要自报年方二八（二乘八等于十六岁），尚未婚配等个人信息。表演强调用规定的动作来表达喜怒哀乐，像发怒时吹胡子甩袖子，动脑筋时用手指头在脑门上划圈，情急时反复搓双手，高兴时高声用假嗓子笑，而且浑身抖动等。看起来京剧的表演程式脱离了实际生活，但它源于生活，高于生活，观众看戏时不但能够进入剧情，而且还得到了艺术的享受。20世纪30年代，京剧艺术大师梅兰芳到前苏联访问演出，苏联戏剧大师斯坦尼司拉夫斯基看了梅兰芳演的《贵妃醉酒》后十分欣赏。斯坦尼的戏剧理论体系是要求生活真实，但台上的杨贵妃嘴巴咬着酒杯前俯后仰，装疯卖傻，一系列虚拟动作，确实把杨贵妃内心的抑郁无望淋漓尽致地表达出来了。斯坦尼没有放过最细微的地方，他甚至观察到梅兰芳的十个手指的动作，认为具有很大的表现力；最后是"打"，就是武打。在京剧的传统保留剧目中，武打戏还是占了一定比例，武生和刀马旦也是一群经过专门训练的艺术人才，他们一般从四五岁开始就接受专业培训，到了成年登台演出，都具备一身功夫，所谓花拳绣腿，在舞台上表演各种高难度动作。

三是表演的抽象性和虚拟性。京剧表演一般都有虚拟的特点。如大幕拉开，台当中只有一张桌子两把椅子，没有布景，有人推门，进门，回身关门，都是用动作来表达。骑马用一条马鞭代替，一只手拿着马鞭就算骑上了马，一边走路一边摇动马鞭，就是骑着马奔跑，把马鞭放下，就算下了马。坐船也同样，当一个人上船，一跳跳到船上，身体要蹲一下，在船那一头的船夫身体要升一下，两个人还要配合一沉一浮，重复几次，然后达到平衡。武打戏中，在双方将领出场前，都有十来个士兵作前导，每一个士兵都代表了千军万马，等等。总的说，京剧用道具很少，甚至不用道具，表演虚拟性例子不胜枚举。

昆　剧

昆剧是京剧诞生以前的一种古老的流行全国的主要剧种，在六百多年前的元代，它最早出现在江苏省的昆山县，是南方许多地方戏曲中的一种，由于有几位戏剧家的创造改进，它很快脱颖而出，影响扩大到江南一带，压倒其他的地方剧种，到400年前的明代中叶，地方官员把昆剧带到京城北京后，立刻在京城流行起来，它不但受到朝廷和上上下下官员的喜爱，还受到老百姓的欢迎。到清代初期，昆剧被

昆剧《墙头马上》

称为"雅部"，在北京城和其他地方一枝独秀，一直到京剧兴起以后其受欢迎的程度才被京剧所取代。

　　昆剧的出现，使中国戏剧在元曲以后达到又一个高峰，第一，它把剧中各种角色进行分工定位，把角色明确地分成生、旦、净、丑四类，在生、旦、净、丑里面还细分各个小类。关于四类角色为什么叫生、旦、净、丑？这个问题讨论了几百年也没有明确结果。人们认为其中"生"和"丑"，望文生义还可以想得通，而"旦"和"净"的名称，确实使人百思不得其解。有人说，"旦"是女人，最早演戏时，她们上场，前面有人挑一担花篮作前导。"净"是花脸，脸上涂满颜料，他们演完戏后，必须把脸洗干净，但这样的解释也未必有说服力。第二，它对各个角色的唱、念、做、打，做了更加程式化的规定，这一点在上面的京剧部分已有详细说明，从这里也可以看到昆剧对以后的京剧的重大影响。第三，昆剧的文字文学性强，韵律清高，它的许多保留剧目都是明、清时代著名剧作家的原创，音乐缠绵婉转，优美动听，演员演唱注重控制声调，咬字吐音清楚，形体舞蹈注意协调和谐。因此，昆剧的整个格调十分高雅，表演细腻，抒情性强，被誉为戏剧百花园中的一支幽香的兰花，传统评论说它"流丽幽远"、"听之最足荡人"。但是也正是由于它的高雅，以后逐渐走向贵族化、宫廷化，脱离大众，因而被京剧取而代之。在京剧兴起的两百多年间，昆剧濒临灭绝，一直到1956年，浙江昆剧团改编演出传统昆剧剧目《十五贯》，在全国产生巨大反响。《十五贯》救活了这支清幽兰花，后来，全国许多省市先后恢复建立了昆剧团，人们又可以经常欣赏到传统昆剧在舞台上的风采。2001年，昆剧被联合国教科文组织授予"人类口头非物质文化代表作"称号。

中国除了京剧和昆剧，还有其他许多地方剧种，这里就不再一一介绍了。现在有不少年轻人，还有外国人，平时不大接触中国传统戏曲，觉得它们不容易看懂，这主要有两方面原因：一是传统剧目的题材大多是一些历史故事，如果他们不知道相关历史背景，看起来就比较吃力；其次，缺乏对传统戏曲的基础知识。这篇关于中国戏剧的文章，就是为了说明怎样欣赏京剧和昆剧，看戏的人有了这些知识，再对剧目的历史背景事先作一点了解，欣赏一出中国传统戏剧应该不会有太大困难了。

Chapter 11
Chinese Opera

Source of Chinese Opera

Chinese traditional opera came into vogue in Yuan Dynasty (1260—1368). Historians attributed the appearance of the opera to two factors: One was the increase of more cities and towns, and the increase of more town people made theaters and storytelling houses spring up. The second, Yuan's Mongolian rulers stopped examining and adopting Han people to be officials, and Han intellectuals had to turned a livelihood for themselves to create Yuan qü-opera. Yuan qü-opera took the inheritance of ci-poetry in Song Dynasty (ci-poems were a kind of rhythmical songs sung popularly among people) Yuan qü-opera writers wrote drama scripts integrating with individual qü-poems in them, just like arias been integrated in western operas. As a result, qü-opera in Yuan Dynasty became the source of Chinese traditional opera, and made Chinese drama show an unique Chinese style of opera at its very beginning. The Yuan qü-poetry and Yuan qü-opera were both the precious literary treasures, and some of the great Yuan qü writers were honored and been listed among a few literary big names in Chinese literature history.

Peking Opera

Peking Opera was the superb quintessence of Chinese culture, from which Chinese people always felt a sense of pride and dignity.

In early Qing Dynasty, in a bid to attend the ceremony of an emperor's 80 birthday, a local opera troupe of Anhui Province went to Peking (Beijing), and its performance was warmly accepted by the emperor and the royal family members (around 1665). Years later, another two Anhui opera troupes and a Hubei Province troupe went to Beijing. The four opera troupes made an exceptionally prosperous occasion in capital stages, and the artists had an opportunity to collect the essence of performing skills. And then shortly afterward, a new kind of opera began to take shape: It was Peking Opera. Peking Opera had showed its three characteristic features:

A scene of Peking Opera

Firstly, every assortment of character roles featured a unified modeling. The character roles in Peking Opera were classified into four categories: "sheng", "dan", "jing", "chou". "Sheng" meant men, including young sheng, old sheng, kung fu sheng; "Dan" meant women, including flowery dan, blue clothes (poor girl), old dan, kung fu dan; "Jing" meant men with heavy colorful make-ups, consisting of a wide range of roles, such as officials, generals (honest and evil), heroes, outlaws, gods and demons. The colors of their make-up represented the role's status: red represented honest, black represented valiant, white face represented treacherous, blue represented ghost and demon, and golden represented god. So, audience could easily distinguish the good from evil of the roles from their facial make-ups. And "chou" meant clown, usually was of low social status, and they unexceptionally got a square of white color painted on the front of their nose.

Secondly, there was a formulistic system in performance. The performing skills of Peking Opera consisted of four parts: "singing", "speaking", "acting" and "playing kung fu". "Singing" was the most essential among the four, and therefore became the most important basic skill for the opera actor and actress. Whenever the story came to a hot point, the actor or actress always sang a lengthy song to reveal his or her inner mind sentiments. And all of the renowned Peking Opera artists over hundreds of years boasted to have the ingenuity and creativity of singing style of his or her own that gave the performance the special appeal. "Speaking" in Peking Opera was also different from that in other drama or film, because the sentence structures were rhythmical, and artists spoke them with modified voice and tone. So speaking rhythmical line was also a basic skill for performing the Opera. "Acting" of Peking Opera was something like dancing. There were a series of fixed formula of body movements to display a variety of feelings and emotions. Usually, when the story began, a man walked with his slow and square steps to the spotlight, taking a seat, and began to introduce his family and career background and current situation, and introduce what kind of trouble he met. If the one was a girl, she would also reveal some private messages like she was now sixteen years old and hadn't yet get married, etc. The most fixed acting formulas were also modified: When a man flied into rages, he blew his beard and swung his sleeves; When the role

Artists apply their make-ups

pondered over something, he pointed and circled a finger on his brain; When a role felt happy, he laughed loud, with a modified sharp voice"Ha, ha, ha!" and all his body was quivered rhythmically. As for "playing kung fu", the kung fu artists would begin their training from 4—6 years old, and when they were of age, they could perform a variety of high quality kung fu feats on the stage.

Thirdly, there were symbolized and imitated motions in performing Peking Opera. Actors used imitated actions to express what he was doing: opening the door, entering the room and locking up the door. When an actor picked up a horse-whip, that symbolized he mounted a horse back. When two generals of two opposite sides came on the stage, there were some soldiers pioneering ahead of them, and every soldier here symbolized tens of thousands of troops …The examples could only be mentioned a few.

Kunjü Opera

Kunjü Opera was a kind of ancient opera dominating stage nationwide for more than 200 years before Peking Opera's appearance. It was originally a local opera in Kunshan County, Jiangsu Province, and began to stand head and shoulders out above others thanked to some wise artists who got it renovated. In mid Ming Dynasty (about 400 years ago) , a local official brought Kunjü Opera to capital Beijing, and immediately won

A Kunjü actress

a wide acclaimation from the audience. Shortly afterward, Kunjü Opera spread to all major cities and enjoyed the situation of "One beauty outshining all other flowers".

Kunjü Opera had exerted a direct impact to Peking Opera. As a matter of fact, the classification of character roles of sheng, dan, jing chou, as well as the formula system of performance in Peking Opera were all inherited from Kunjü Opera. More, Kunjü Opera's songs, drama scripts and actors' lines all boasted of their high literary values, and the artists' singing and performing were particular about nobleness in flavor and exquisiteness in quality. Critics held that Kunjü Opera was "a cymbidium with gentle fragrance", and the singing of Kunjü Opera sounded "to have special affection and captivity". But, just due to its refined taste, Kunjü Opera took a road toward ivory tower catering distinguished class and lost its appeal among mass people, and finally it was replaced by Peking Opera. During 200 years of Peking Opera thriving, Kunjü Opera had fallen down on the verge of extinguishment. It was in 1956, Zhejiang Kunjü Opera troupe rehearsed a traditional Kunjü Opera play *15 Strings of Coins* and put it on the stage, that proved a big success, resulting in "one play rescued a sort of opera surviving". Since then, new Kunjü Opera troupes were set up in most of provinces, rehearsing and performing traditional Kunjü Opera plays, and won great appeal to both domestic and international audiences.

音乐舞蹈的起源

音乐舞蹈在原始社会就有了，音乐和舞蹈，两者如影随形，从一开始就是结合在一起的。史书记载最早有葛天氏之歌，葛天氏社会是比黄帝、炎帝更早的一个太平年代，人民丰衣足食，葛天氏之歌是三个人一组，拉着牛尾巴边唱边跳，自娱自乐。其次，中国的音乐舞蹈还和诗歌结合在一起，据记载，有一个老农在田里一边劳动，一边用农具拍打土地，一边高唱山歌：

日出而作，日落而息，凿井而饮，耕田而食，帝力于我何有哉。

这首歌词朴实优美，艺术性很高，所以被认为是中国有记载的最早的一首诗歌，歌词意思说，我们凭劳动吃饭，帝王对我们有什么用呢？

再有，中国古时候音乐还和庆典及祭神祭祖结合在一起，像另外一首早期诗歌：

卿云烂兮，纠缦缦兮，日月光辉，旦复旦兮。

传说舜传位给禹，在庄重的典礼上，由舜领头，大家唱起这首雄壮的歌。这首歌的文学价值也很高，意思是说，云彩灿烂，像洁白的布伸展开来，日月光辉，一个早晨又一个早晨，永远照临大地。他们歌颂英明的帝王一代一

甩袖舞彩陶俑

111

代地传下去。另外还有传说，每次当舜演奏音乐，各种野兽都会跑来，围在旁边一动不动地静听。

这里再说一个音乐舞蹈和诗歌相结合的例子：战国时期，齐国宰相孟尝君养着食客三千，鸡鸣狗盗之徒也纷纷投到门下，有一天来了一个叫冯谖的人，孟尝君问他有什么技能，回答说没有技能，孟尝给了他最低的待遇。过了不久，冯谖弹起铗来（铗是带剑鞘的剑，弹铗是一种舞蹈动作），他一边弹铗，一边唱道："长铗归来乎，食无鱼。"意思是说，长铗呀，我们回家吧，呆在这里没有鱼吃，于是孟尝给了他鱼吃。接着他又弹了两次铗，一次提出，出门要坐车，另一次提出要钱养母亲，孟尝先后都满足了他的要求。评论家说，"长铗归来乎"五个字是中国古诗中最短的一首诗。后来事实证明，冯谖是一个非凡的能人。

制礼作乐和礼崩乐坏

上古时候，音乐用来祭祀天地祖先，所以它是很高尚圣洁的，例如古琴是原始部族领袖炎帝制造的：琴身长360寸，代表一年360天，高6寸，代表东南西北上下六个方向，琴的顶部是半圆的，代表天，底部是平的，代表地。到了周代初期，音乐被放在一个十分重要的位置，成为治理国家，对人民进行思想道德教育的重要工具。统治者"制礼作乐"，就是制定了森严的等级制度和人民的行为规范，同时用音乐来教化人民思想，引导社会风气，使得人民个个有高尚的道德，社会秩序井井有条，因此出现了一个太平盛世。数百年后，国家开始动乱，到了春秋时代，孔夫子眼看天下大乱，民不聊生，认为这都是由于"礼崩乐坏"的缘故，当时发生了一件"礼崩乐坏"的典型例子：鲁国宰相家里"八佾舞于庭"（佾，一排人，八佾意思是八排舞女），孔子知道了痛心疾首，说："是可忍也，孰不可忍也。"就是说，这件事可以容忍，还有什么事不可容忍？但这到底是件什么事值得这样大惊小怪呢？原来按礼的规定，皇帝在宫廷看跳舞可用八佾，诸侯王用六佾，诸侯国的宰相只能用四佾，现在鲁国宰相在家看跳舞用八佾，不是岂有此理吗？另一件事与此相仿，当时的郑国（今河南中部）老百姓唱民歌很普遍，青年男女常常聚在一起对歌，孔子听说也大为恼火，责备说是"郑声淫"（音乐有伤风化），说是亡国之音。

春秋战国出现礼崩乐坏，说明音乐舞蹈开始从崇高庙堂里走了出来，功能开始分

古代编钟

化。第一类，它继续走和诗歌相结合的道路。从汉初开始，朝廷设立了专门管理音乐舞蹈的机构，叫乐府。当时乐府的主管是个有名的音乐家，他除了负责操办宫廷礼仪音乐外，主要搜集诗歌和民歌，配上乐曲，为皇帝进行歌舞表演，这部分诗歌被称为乐府诗。到了唐代，乐府机构更加庞大，诗歌被配上乐曲越来越多，同时也在民间广泛传唱。乐府诗后来还转化成宋词元曲，元曲是中国戏曲的起源，所以，今天的传统戏曲，仍旧和音乐舞蹈诗歌紧密结合在一起。

音乐舞蹈的另一支向娱乐消遣方向发展，在这方面，史料有不少有趣的记载，像"曲有误，周郎顾"的故事，说三国时期吴国的军事统帅周瑜，年轻英俊，深通音律，他每次听到演奏乐器的女孩弹错一个音符，一定要叫停，然后亲自给予纠正，所以后来不少姑娘故意地"为得周郎顾，时时误拨弦"，传为美谈。也从这时候开始，私人蓄养歌舞伎的风气逐渐蔓延，到了唐代，富贵人家，长期养着歌舞伎的比比皆是，朱门深宅，夜夜弦管歌舞，十分普遍。这里特别要提一下音乐和知识分子的关系，对知识分子来说，弹琴，是他们的一门基本功，也是他们娱乐消遣的一个主要途径，但是，他们弹琴的同时也是为了修身养性，像乐曲的主题大多是高山流水，明月清风，孤云野鹤，尤其是在弹的时候，环境要很清静，或是在月光下，或是在竹林里，旁边还要焚一炉香，他们通过弹琴来过滤掉世俗杂念，做到清心寡欲。所以在知识分子眼里，音乐是一种高雅艺术，如果离开了高雅品位，音乐堕落成为靡靡之音，就为人们所不齿了。不过事情总是有例外，汉代文学家司马相如有一次到大富商卓家作客，卓有个女儿名叫文君，长得十分漂亮，司马相如在晚饭以后抚琴一曲，用琴声挑逗她，半夜里，卓文君来到司马相如房间，两人连夜一起私奔了。司马相如弹靡靡之音，抱得美人归，人们不以为非，反而认为这是有情人终成眷属，成为音乐史上一段佳话。

第三类的音乐舞蹈存在于广阔陇陌之间，流行于草根农民之中。有一文章说，战国后期，有一个音乐家在楚国京城的闹市区，唱起通俗歌曲《下里巴人》，引来数千人大合唱，后来当他唱起高雅歌曲《阳春白雪》，大家一哄而散，跟着他唱的只剩十来个人。楚国处在湖南、湖北、四川一带，那里农民向来有热爱歌舞的传统，到了唐代，诗人刘禹锡被皇帝下放到这里做地方官，他立刻被农民蓬蓬勃勃的歌舞活动吸引住了，那里的老百姓在举行各种大小集会以及逢年过节时，都要唱民歌，许多村子里，人们唱歌还伴随舞蹈。山歌村笛虽然显得有点粗鄙，但它带有一股泥土芬芳，刘禹锡得到启发和鼓舞，也写了许多民歌，后来有一天，他走过田头，看到有一群农民正挥舞竹枝，边唱边舞，他一问，这民歌曲子名字叫竹枝词，他就把自己写的民歌取名为《竹枝词》。数年后，刘禹锡带着《竹枝词》回到京城，立刻引起轰动，《竹枝词》带有芳草清香的歌词和曲调，像一枝异常鲜艳的花朵，绽放在唐代诗坛的百花园里。

多民族音乐舞蹈融合

汉代开通丝绸之路，新疆的少数民族音乐舞蹈随之传入中土，到唐代，边疆的地方官为了迎合皇帝的爱好，不断把带有异域情调的音乐和乐器介绍进来，不久它们就在全国流传，最著名的有"凉州曲"、"甘州曲"、"伊州曲"等。"凉州曲"的音调十分凄楚，史料记载，有一个官员乘船到扬州，晚上停歇在船舶拥挤的渡口旁边，月亮升上来，他站在船头，用笛子吹起"凉州曲"，只吹了第一声，周围立刻安静下来，他继续吹一会，旁边的旅客和船工都低下了头，再过一会，许多听的人都哭泣起来，有的还哭出声音。关于少数民族的音乐，唐代有不少诗人记述了自己听后的感受，像诗人李顾对一个来自新疆的少数民族音乐家吹奏龟兹乐赞扬备至："枯桑老柏寒飕飕，九雏鸣凤乱啾啾，龙吟虎啸一时发，万籁百泉相与秋……变调如同杨柳春，上林繁花照眼新。"李顾的几首欣赏音乐的诗写得很有精神。

这里特别要说一说多民族歌舞集大成的剧目《霓裳羽衣舞》，也叫《霓裳羽衣曲》，作者是唐代风流才子皇帝唐玄宗，歌舞领衔主演杨贵妃。玄宗在皇宫里建立了一个庞大的歌舞班子，就是有名的梨园，里面作曲、唱歌、跳舞、乐器演奏等人才俱全，乐工有三百多人，加上舞蹈演员数百人，他们的乐器也融合了汉族本土乐器和外来的少数民族乐器，像琴、筝、琵琶、磬（铜质打击乐器）、羯鼓、箫、笛、箜篌等，济济一堂（胡琴到后来才传入）。据史料说，有一个将军领兵到新疆打仗，全军覆没，依法要治重罪，但他收集到一首新疆歌曲，非常优美，他把它献给玄宗，玄宗龙颜大悦，非但不罚他，还重重奖赏了他。玄宗就是用这个曲子为基调，创作了《霓裳羽衣曲》，同时，玄宗还亲自教人歌舞，教乐工演奏，整个剧目分三十六段，演出六小时。人们可以想一想当时的盛况，整个演出恢宏大气，充满幻觉和异国情调，音乐时而抒情，时而奔放，舞蹈演员个个打扮成仙女，婆娑起舞，边舞边歌。可惜，这样一个令人神往的剧目今天已经失传了，《霓裳羽衣舞》在中国音乐舞蹈史上留下了一个传奇、一个高峰。

音乐舞蹈同戏剧相结合

从元代开始，中国出现了戏剧。戏剧家所编写的剧本多数是历史和人物传奇故事，当中有对话，也有唱段，唱段的文字优美，富有韵味，演员要经过长期专门训练，表演要具备唱、念、做、打四门功夫。在这四门功夫中，唱有乐器伴奏，很清楚属于音乐范畴，而做和打，展现形体动作美，属舞蹈范畴，所以，中国戏剧是把文学、戏剧、音乐、舞蹈等因素融于一体。清代出现京剧，仍旧继承唱念做打传统，而人物脸谱更规范化，表演更程式化。也许戏剧表演的故事情节更能吸引人，在这以后的两百多年来，在城镇正规的剧场舞台上，京剧和地方戏曲一直占据着统治地位，中国的真正的音乐剧和舞蹈剧没有得到很好发展，像唐代《霓裳羽衣舞》这样大型的真正意义上的舞蹈剧，只是昙花一现，以后再也没有见到了。一直到近代，随着西方戏剧音乐舞蹈样式的传入，京剧和地方戏曲的一统天下局面被打破，中国的音乐舞蹈才发生新的变化，近几十年来有了长足发展。

不过在广大农村，农民一直有着自己的音乐舞蹈。龙舞是最有代表性的一种民间舞蹈，三千多年前就有了，一直风行全国。在长江以南地区，民间还流行狮子舞、

民间的花灯舞

花鼓、打莲湘、旱地船、大和尚背花姑娘等；北方地区则有秧歌、腰鼓、高跷和红绸舞等。各种舞蹈都有乐器伴奏，打击乐像锣鼓，吹奏乐像笛子、唢呐，声音热烈而高亢。每当传统节日或逢喜事，兴高采烈的人们汇集拢来，排成队伍，一边走，一边表演，尤其在春节元宵节等场合，人们除了表演歌舞，还举行化装游行，像北方有些地方腰鼓队，游行时全体都要戴上面具，化装成天上金刚大力士，用来驱逐恶鬼，古人有诗这样说："道人劝我清明来，腰鼓百面如春雷。"

Chapter 12
Music And Dance

Enacting Etiquette And Esteeming Music

People in ancient era considered the music as a sacred thing, as they played music while holding rituals to pay worship to the Heaven or their forbears. In 1100 BC, the founder emperor of Zhou Dynasty created a peaceful and harmonious world by carrying out a policy of "enacting etiquette and esteeming music". The rulers applied music as an ideological weapon to promote people's moral integrity and keep social order effectively.

Four hundred years later, the country became unrest and chaotic. The independent sub-states launched wars to conquer each other, and people suffered a life of dire disaster. Confucius put blames for the matter to "etiquette falling and music degrading", and he made his efforts in every possible ways in an attempt that he could draw the country back to the peaceful world 400 hundred years ago by making a fresh start of the "etiquette and music" policy. But he was finally failed.

Etiquette Falling And Music Degrading

The phenomenon of "etiquette falling and music degrading" indicated a fact that the music began to step out from its sacred palace and reversed its functions. The music functions began to divide into three parts:

Firstly, the music began to be blended with poetry, dance and folk song, and finally became an integrated part of Chinese opera. The government of Tang Dynasty founded a special institution named "Jiao Fang" in charge of collecting music and dance resources, as well as training music talents, providing

Geisha in Tang Dynasty

117

entertainments for the emperor. (see more in following part)

The second, people began to develop the function of music and dance as a form of relaxing and recreation. In Tang Dynasty, it began prevailing for many rich families to keep geishas and hold singing and dancing parties for entertainment. It became a common scene that the sounds of singing and the shadows of dancing were seen and heard from grand residences and gardens after night setting in. In addition, as for intellectuals, most of them had "four favored hobbies" or "four basic skills" for their leisure activities, i.e., playing music instruments, playing chess, brushing calligraphy and splashing painting. They also availed themselves of the four skills, especially playing music instrument "qin", to mold and refine their temperaments. The music subjects they played usually related with lonely moon and clean wind, solitary clouds and wild crane, or blue maintain and green water. They also seated a quiet and secluded site, under the moon or inside the bamboo forest, and resorting play music to wash away their everyday worldly thinking. They always told off the popular entertaining music as "vulgar taste".

The third kind of music and dance was prevailing in wide countryside and among mass peasants. In Hunan and Sichuan provinces, there existed profound tradition of performing folk song and dance created by peasants themselves. Liu Yuxi, an outstanding poet in mid Tang Dynasty, when he was exiled to the places to be a local official, saw peasants perform singing and dancing in every occasion they spent holidays and festivals. The folk song and dance sprayed out sweet smelling of grass and soil that enriched the poet's inspirations. He became enthusiastic to collect folk songs that helped him achieve big to create poems rich in folk song taste.

Multi-Ethnic Music And Dance

There were many ethnic minority people living around Chinese mainland through thousands of years. The minorities outside the western and northern border were nomads, and their people were mostly good at both singing and dancing. Chinese Han majority in mainland had exchanged their culture and civilization with ethnic minorities through the famous Silk Road that started from Xi'an City, Shaanxi Province going westward to Xinjiang, where stayed a variety of ethnic minority people. In Tang Dynasty, many officials in border area, for the sake of seeking favor from the emperor, always collected and introduced minorities' music and instruments to offer to the emperors. And shortly afterward, the ethnic minorities' music and instruments became popular among Han people. There were many stories recorded by historians, poems composed by poets, describing vividly how the ethnic minority music been warmly accepted by Han people. It's said, in Tang Dynasty, a military commander was disastrously defeated in a battle by minority troops in Xinjiang, and faced a fatal punishment. But things turned out to be contrary, he finally got a great reward. Why? It was because he had collected a beautiful minority music. The emperor was very delighted at the hearing of the music that he had never appreciated before. The emperor was Xuanzong, an emperor popular for his romantic stories with his Concubine Yang Yuhuan. The emperor kept a large scale of singing and dancing troupe named "Li Yuan" (literally meaning pear garden) in his forbidden city, including 300 more musicians, hundreds of singers and dancers. Xuanzong, by make use of the new music, created a historically-famous singing and dancing opera titled *Nishangyuyi Dance* (literally cloudy skirts and feathery clothes). Its leading dancer was Concubine Yang Yuhuan. The opera appeared really an outstanding arts work with a distinct exotic flavor. The dancing performance was divided into 36 episodes, lasting for six hours, displaying a gigantic atmosphere of splendidness and fantasy. The opera *Nishangyuyi Dance* left behind its honorable and prestigious name in Chinese arts history.

Music And Dance Integrated into Opera

The dancing opera *Nishangyuyi Dance* had simply come and gone. Since then, there never appeared another singing and dancing opera alike anymore. In fact, the real sing and dance arts hadn't well developed in Chinese arts history, instead, the traditional

Chinese Music

119

opera seemed like to be much more cherished by Chinese people as the opera usually had interesting and intriguing stories. Chinese traditional opera was originated from Yuan Dynasty, and its representative works were Kunjü Opera and Peking Opera. The opera scripts consisted of rhythmical dialogue and song, and its performance consisted of a series of formulistic system: singing, speaking, acting and playing Kung fu. (see detailed relations in previous chapter 11)

But, along with the process of cultural exchanges between china and western world in recent 100 years, China saw a variety of modern western arts styles coming in. As a result, a lot of Chinese young people preferred to accept western style of arts, like modern drama, western opera, western dance and western symphony, and Chinese traditional opera was left in limbo. Young people (foreigners as well) felt Chinese tradition opera seemed hard to understand. It was probably due to Chinese opera usually had a historical story they didn't know, as well as had a series of complicated performing formulas. So, they could at first refer to the explanations of chapter 11, that helped them understand Chinese opera's performing formulas. They could also learn the historical story from synopsis. And then they could surely appreciate Chinese opera effectively.

中　国　菜

中国人的美食传统

　　人类烹调食物，首先要有火，中国有个传统说法是燧人氏钻木取火，燧人氏大约生活在距今五千年的三皇五帝时期，而实际上，中国的原始人开始用火的时间要早很多。考古学家于1929年，在北京周口店挖掘出北京猿人头盖骨的同时，还发现那里有一处很厚的储灰层，证明那时北京猿人已经能够取得并保存火种。北京猿人距今七十万年左右，这也是迄今为止，人们发现的中国先民最早用火并且开始熟食的记录。

　　先民用火有三个发展阶段。最早的办法最简单，就是在一块大石头上点燃起篝火，把食料放在火上一起烧，叫石烹，石烹有时候在食料外面包一层树叶泥土，防止烧焦；第二阶段是水烹，用一张牛皮盛食料，加点水，然后把一堆小石头烧热，丢进牛皮里，不断地丢进取出石头，把食料煨熟；第三阶段，先民发明了陶器，时间大约在距今一万年到八千年之间，陶器可以架在火上烧，传热功能更好，烹煮范围大大扩展，并且可以使用调味品。陶器的使用，表明真正意义上的烹饪的出现，人类的饮食文明实现又一次飞跃，这一次

古代的食器（鬲）

飞跃的意义，不亚于火的发明和使用。

事实上，饮食是人们生活中第一件大事，史书上有无数关于中国人喜欢美食的记载，有的还变成了成语。以孔子为例，他一生事事以身作则，但他并不提倡吃苦为乐，而是讲究享受，他的学生说他"食不厌精，脍不厌细"（吃得越精美越好，肉加工越细越好），这样，老师作出榜样，"食不厌精"变成了一句成语。后世有一个读书人坦白承认，对于孔老夫子的所有教导，他都做不到，只有一样做到了，就是"食不厌精，脍不厌细"。孟子也是一个美食家，有一次，他的学生公孙丑问他："脍炙与羊枣孰美？（脍炙是烧肉丝，羊枣是山东出产的一种小甜枣，这是问烧肉丝和甜枣哪个好吃）"孟子回答很干脆："脍炙哉！（烧肉丝好吃啊）"因为烧肉丝人人爱吃，所以，从这里又引申出一个成语"脍炙人口"。到了三国时期，曹植才高八斗，不但诗文盖世，同时也是一个美食家。有一天他组织一个打猎队伍浩浩荡荡上山打猎，打猎结束，满载而归，在一个叫平乐的地方举行宴会，这次打猎和宴会由于他写的一首诗而被传诵千古："归来宴平乐，美酒斗十千，脍鲤臇胎虾，炮鳖炙熊蹯，鸣俦啸匹侣，列坐竟长筵……"这里前面的"美酒斗十千"成为一句成语，最后两句是形容宴会上的热闹气氛，而当中两句充分显示了当时菜肴的丰富和烹调方法的多样化。这里短短十个字都没有罗列菜名，只是列举鲤鱼、虾、鳖和熊掌四样东西，很有代表性，尤其是四样东西各有不同烹调方法，这非常形象地说明了，早在一千八百多年前，或许还要早得多，中国的美食和菜肴的烹调技术，已经达到了一个很高的水平。

中国菜的特色

中国还有一个"美食方丈"的成语，说早在春秋战国时期，诸侯王的餐桌有一丈见方（3.3×3.3米），上面摆满菜肴，算起来应该有一百盘，不知是否夸张了，但清代宫廷有一种叫满汉全席的，参加宴会的有数千人之多，场面非常浩大，这是确有其事的。关于烹调的书籍，历代创作也很丰富，但时间久了很多已经失传，现在最著名的是清代文学家袁枚写的《随园食单》，里面系统介绍了自古以来烹调技术的发展，记载了元、明、清三代流行的菜肴342种。这些事实说明，中国的菜肴确是一种洋洋大观的文化，它的花色品种之多、口味之丰富，世界上没有哪个民族可以企及。中国菜

满汉全席

肴的特点有以下三方面：

第一，中国菜肴原料包罗万象，凡是天上飞的，水里游的，地上跳的爬的，山珍海味，没有哪一样被轻易放过。像吃蛇，以前是广东人风俗，现在全国各地的人都吃了。现在中国人爱吃海鲜，并且有一种理论，说是四条腿（牛羊猪）不如两条腿（鸡鸭），两条腿不如没有腿（鱼虾）。许多人吃肉不喜欢吃大块肉，像猪蹄、鸡鸭翅膀、脖子、爪子等，它们往往比大块的肉畅销。还有，人们把有的原料改造，变成另外口味，像把动物小腿的筋抽出来，晒干，再经过发泡加工，就变成另外一种原料"蹄筋"，用蹄筋可以做出许多不同花色的菜肴来。同样，把原来不大受欢迎的猪皮收集起来，晒干，经过大油锅炸，就变成松软清香的原料"肉皮"，用肉皮也能烹调出许多种风味菜和家乡菜。

第二，烹调方法多样性和精工细作，是中国菜的另一个主要特色。烹调方法全世界差不多，主要有煨、焖、蒸、炒、烘、炸等等，而中国厨师特别擅长蒸和炒。蒸是把原料放在蒸笼里隔水蒸熟，它能保持食品的原汁原味。炒的方法西方人用得比较少，尤其是一般家庭，不喜欢炒菜时满屋油烟，但炒菜正是中国烹调的精髓。炒菜时掌握油温十分关键，锅里油温最高可达200℃—230℃，油冒青烟，食料下去噼啪有声。油温分三个等级，什么菜用什么油温，不能马虎。其次是油用多少，是大油锅还是小油锅，厨师们往往把原料先放进大油锅烫一遍，再用另外小锅子炒，当然，掌握

123

好炒的时间也很重要。概括来说，炒菜学问在掌握火候，就是火的大小，油温的高低，炒的时间，这当中有一样弄不好，就会影响菜肴的美味。炒菜还有一个绝招，厨师在炒的时候，往往会突然锅内锅外大火烧起来，这不是"意外"，而是一种烹调方法，叫"明火"，经过明火烧出来的菜肴有一种不一般的味道。所以，往往有许多专业厨师，到了休息日带一家人上馆子吃饭，其中一个重要原因，就是馆子里的厨房条件，像大油锅高油温等，一般家庭不具备，因此，任是烹饪高手，在家庭小厨房里，水平就难以发挥了。

关于中国菜肴的精工细作也是人所共知，但是到底精细到什么程度，现在引用《红楼梦》里的一段描写，它可以给人们一个具体而生动的印象，那就是刘姥姥在大观园里吃茄子的故事：刘姥姥白吃了半天茄子，还不知道是什么东西，听说是茄子，就问怎么做法，回去自己也可以做，凤姐告诉她，用新鲜茄子削去皮，切成丁，在鸡油里炸过，再拿鸡肉、笋、蘑菇、香豆腐干，也切成丁，放在一起，在鸡汤里煨，汤汁收干后，加点香油，收藏起来，等到要吃时拿出来，再用一点鸡肉丁拌一拌就好了。刘姥姥听了连连吐舌头，说："阿弥陀佛，这点茄子要配上几只鸡啊。"这一碟茄子在贾家只能算是一道普通菜，不知道高级菜会奢侈到什么样子，从这里可以看出，中国人为了口味不惜代价，做起来无所不用其极。

第三，色、香、味。中国菜肴素有色香味俱全的美誉，但还应该加两个字："形"和"名"。形就是菜肴造型很美，许多简直像是艺术品，名就是每盘菜肴都有一个漂亮名字，所以准确地说，应该是体现色、香、味、形、名五字原则。例如烧一条鱼，厨师把鱼身上的肉切成细条，经过油炸后，样子像一朵盛开的金黄色菊花，这盘菜的名字就叫"菊花鳜鱼"；另如烧汤，厨师用鸡蛋做成一朵朵小荷花，浮在水面上，旁边放莼菜当做荷叶，叫"绿云扶荷花"；江南还有一个名菜"叫花子鸡"，加工很讲究，把整只鸡洗干净后，在

中国菜

鸡肚子里塞进调料香料，鸡的外面包一张大荷叶，扎紧，外面再裹一层泥土，然后用火烤，烤得骨酥肉烂，打开时，鸡肉香气扑鼻，除了烧烤香以外，还带有一股荷叶清香，据说这个菜的原创者是常常偷鸡摸狗的叫花子们，所以今天的菜名仍旧保留了他们的专利。

四大菜系

中国菜有四大菜系之分，即，北京菜系、淮扬菜系、四川菜系和广东菜系，它们正好代表四个大区域，北京菜系代表北方，淮扬菜系代表华东，四川菜系代表西部，广东菜系代表华南。它们各自有什么特点呢？

持蟹赏菊图

北京菜系：历史上元、明、清三个朝代连续在北京建都，王侯将相达官贵人云集，这里的菜肴保留了唐宋朝代的传统，同时吸收了历史悠久的山东菜的精华，还掺杂了北方少数民族的传统口味。北京菜的特点是，擅长爆、炒、熘、烤、炸、扒，烹调肉食讲究鲜嫩滑爽，加工山珍海味讲究用比较重的调味品。近几十年来，北京烤鸭和北京涮羊肉成了著名招牌菜，誉满海内外。

淮扬菜系：淮是江苏北部的淮河流域，扬是扬州市。自从隋炀帝开通大运河以来，扬州地处大运河进入长江的交通要道，千百年来一直是个繁华的商业城市，酒楼鳞次栉比，人们享受消费，推动了饮食业持续兴旺发展。淮扬菜特点是，特别重视色香味，口味清淡，鲜而不腻，有点甜，讲究每种食物保持自身风味，用调味品较少，原汁原味。

四川菜系：四川盆地沃野千里，气候变化大，物产品类丰富，一向被称为天府之国，另外四川由于地理环境因素，在历史上战争破坏较少，社会比较稳定，这也直接促成这里饮食文化的繁荣，在烹调风味上独树一帜。四川菜的最大特色是带麻辣味，因调味品搭配不同，分鱼香味型、怪味型、椒麻型、麻辣味型、芥末味型等。现在四川菜以其独特口味，赢得海内外广大美食家的普遍青睐。

广东菜系：广东北有五岭，南临大海，地处珠江流域，土地肥沃，加上气候属亚热带，因此物产特别丰富多样。广东人有酷爱美食的传统，这也因历史上战乱较少，明代以后，海运贸易蓬勃发展，促进广州等沿海城市饮食业的兴隆和繁荣。广东菜的特点是，吃的东西广泛，有"脊背朝天均可食"的说法（什么都吃），加工精细，讲究色香味，爆炒注意三分生，蔬菜色泽嫩绿，尤其擅长烹调鱼类和各种羹汤。

社会发展到今天，中国四大菜系早已超越了本土地域，在全国各个大小城市，四大菜系的酒楼餐馆遍地开花，应有尽有，特别是近些年来，随着饮食业内部的激烈竞争，大家不断推出创新菜肴，各个菜系已经出现互相渗透现象，有许多菜肴已经分不清哪是哪个菜系了。

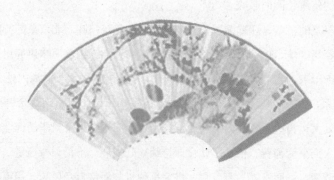

Chapter 13

Chinese Food

Tradition of Chinese Cuisine

Chinese people had a long-lasting tradition of enjoying gourmand food. There were many interesting gourmand stories that afterward became popular idioms. An idiom went: "ten square feet of gourmand food", relating a story of an emperor of sub-state in the Spring & Autumn Period (770—476 BC) whose dining table was as large as 10 square feet. It was calculated that the table could set out as many as more than 100 dishes. The great sage Confucius was also a most discriminating gourmand in history. One of his students said on a book, describing: "He made efforts in every possible way to cook his food perfect and delicious." (also became an idiom) So, a Confucius' disciple in later generation had once owned up that he could do nothing of the sage's teachings but carrying out the "perfect food" instruction. Cao Zhi, a top literary talent in the Three Kingdom Period (220 AD—280) had composed a famous and splendid poem describing vividly a carnival of exciting hunting and ensuing feast. His great-taste delis on the feast included carp, shrimps, soft-shelled turtle and bear's foot sole, by using of various cooking ways as frying, steaming, stewing and roasting. Yuan Mei, a famous man of letters in Qing Dynasty (1644—1911) wrote a book about Chinese cuisine, collecting as many as 342 dishes of food from Yuan (1260—1368) lasting to Ming and Qing dynasties, as well as their cooking ways. The authentic and wide-inclusive book displayed Chinese cuisine was really a precious and rare treasure of Chinese cultural tradition.

Features of Chinese Cuisine

Chinese food, famous for its exclusive style and taste, differed from the food of any other nations and areas in the world. There were three distinguishing features in Chinese food:

The first was its all-inclusive food materials. To say the truth, Chinese ate anything, anything flying over the sky, running on the land and swimming in the water, including cat, dog, snake ... and even animal's internal organs. In the past, only beggars or vagrants

Chinese food

poached dog sometime to allay their hunger, but after the declaration of some scientific research asserting that the dog meat is very nourishing, that provoked a vogue of eating dog in recent years. More, Chinese people were good at remaking one food material into another food material. For example, people take out tendon out from animal's (usually cow and pig) legs, and make it into a new kind of food after some processing. The other is pig's skin. People cut divided the skin, dry and leaven it, and fry it in the hot oil, and then make it a new kind of food material.

The second was special and varied cooking ways. Boiling, steaming, stewing, braising and roasting are the common cooking ways used by chefs all over the world, but Chinese chefs seemed to be most skillful to steaming and stir-frying. Steaming was steaming food in the pot or steamer, that could make the food maintain best the original taste, but in fact, stir-frying turned out to be Chinese chefs' special feat. When doing stir-frying, chefs must handle perfectly three key controlling: controlling flame heating, oil temperature and cooking time. The food taste would be damaged in case of anything wrong with the three key steps. More, there was an exclusive way that chefs always make flame burning up fiercely inside and outside the cooker. It's a special feat of stir-frying, called "burning up a surface flame", rather than a terrible accident. The food taste cooked from the "surface flame" would become extra delicious. It was said many good chefs worked with big restaurants would go eating in restaurants on holidays with their family members. Why they don't cook good food in their own homes? Because they usually lack of cooking conditions required in their homes.

The third was that Chinese food put stress on three words: color, taste and aroma. But it seemed necessary to add additional two words: shape and name, as a Chinese dish was usually beautifully decorated and being given a fine-sounding name. For example, when a chef cooked a mandarin fish, he would prepare the fish by cutting it in a meticulous way, and the fish would come out a shape resembling a yellow blossoming chrysanthemum after frying it in the hot oil. The dish was entitled a good name as "blossoming chrysanthemum mandarin fish". The other example was: when a chef cooked soap, he used eggs to make some lotus flowers, then added water shields around them. The soap was entitled "leaves prop up flowers". There was a time-honored dish

Chinese dining table

named "beggar's chicken" having prevailed hundreds of years in Yangtze Delta area. Chefs cleaned the chicken, put seasoning and spice inside and out, packed it with a large lotus leaf, then roasted it. When the chicken was unpacked, it was crispy outside and soft inside with wonderful sweet-smelling, just mouth-watering. The dish's name indicated the beggar was its first inventor.

Four Food Factions

China had four food factions: Beijing food faction, Yangzhou food faction, Sichuan food faction and Guangdong food faction. The four factions represented China's four big regions: Beijing represented North China, Yangzhou represented Eastern China, Sichuan represented Western China, and Guangdong represented Southern China.

Beijing food faction: Beijing had been the capital of latest three imperial dynasties (Yuan, Ming, Qing) through 650 years. Beijing food consisted of the fined tradition of imperial family as well as the flavor of northern ethnic minorities. Now, "Beijing roasted duck" and "sliced ram Mongolian pot" were the two dishes best known for people both from home and abroad.

Yangzhou food faction: Yangzhou, situated at the traffic hub of Yangtze River and the Great Canal, was a thriving commercial city through 1,500 years, and the high consumption demands made the catering industry kept booming. Yangzhou food featured keeping food original taste and juice, and denying too greasy or strongly flavored.

Sichuan food faction: Sichuan food had its special flavor and taste that won its appeal among most of gourmand people. The characteristics of Sichuan food was its hot chili taste, and the chili taste was also divided into several different types according to the chili combining with other different spices: chili-pepper-sesame, chili-prickly, chili-mustard, chili-garlic-ginger, etc.

Guangdong food faction: Guangdong was a land rich in varied food resources due to its weather and geographical advantages, and its people had a long-lasting tradition of enjoying gourmand food. Guangdong food was usually cooked in a special meticulous way and particular about color, taste and aroma. The chefs were mostly skillful to cook seafood and a variety of soap.

In fact, the appearance of different food factions was caused because China's lands were isolated from each other in ancient time. Now, along with the improvement of economy and people livelihood, recent years saw restaurants of different food factions opening side by side in the same city or even on the same street. Competition was fierce, that provoked new food designs keeping coming forth. It seemed that the bounds of the four food factions have now been constantly broken, and their difference in flavor and taste could be softened and disappeared at last.

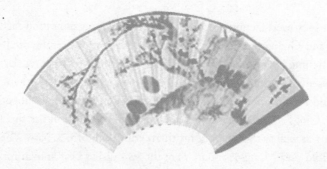

茶 和 酒

第十四篇

茶的传统

中国是最早发明种茶、加工茶、饮茶的国家，中国种茶历史悠久，茶叶的生产和消费数量都为世界之最。中国人喜欢喝茶，热爱喝茶，茶在中国人民的生活中具有特别重要的地位。中国有这样一句老话：老百姓开门七件事，柴、米、油、盐、酱、醋、茶。关于中国茶的历史，大概可分三个阶段：

早在三千多年前，就有四川农民把茶叶进贡给周武王的史料记载，茶叶最早产地在四川，秦汉时逐步向全国移植。历史上记录有许多帝王嗜好饮茶，像三国时代的吴国君主孙皓，他在每年春天采摘新茶的时候，都要开宫廷宴会，邀请大臣们参加，酒席上要求每个人必须"饮酒七升"。其中有这样一个情节，有一个大臣不会喝酒，孙皓就悄悄让他以茶代酒，这就是"以茶代酒"的最早先例。在帝王倡导下，社会上饮茶之风也很快兴盛起来。

在距今一千五百年前的南北朝时期，中国的茶叶生产和消费出现突破性进展。在这以前，茶叶是不加工的，因为茶树春夏秋三季都长新叶，人们一般都是一边从茶树上采下茶叶，一边用茶叶煮水喝，叫茶羹。南北朝时，有人开始把茶叶烘干，制成茶饼，要喝茶时掰一点下来，用水

茶叶制作工场

131

煮或泡。经过加工，干燥的茶叶不但更香更可口，更重要的是，它大大方便了保存和携带，方便了茶叶的买卖流通，从而扩大了茶叶市场，回过来再促进茶叶的出产。史料记载，在唐代，全国各地已经出现许多大大小小的手工制茶作坊，茶叶市场规模也越来越大，当时军队还用茶叶和少数民族换优良马匹。在这同时，茶叶开始销往国外，在南北朝时，就有土耳其商人通过丝绸之路，把茶叶运到土耳其，再转运到阿拉伯和欧洲。

唐代以后，随着各地区加工茶叶方法的多样化，茶叶的花色品种也多了起来，茶叶不只是做成茶饼，还加工成碎片，不仅有经过发酵的茶，还出现了绿茶。到了宋代，有一种风俗大大促进了茶叶质量的提高，这就是"斗茶"盛会。"斗茶"由朝廷倡导，每年在京城开封举行，全国各地产茶区，都把他们最好的茶叶带来，先是展览，然后冲泡，由专家们进行评比，评出当年最佳茶叶。这和现在的选超女好男，选各种宠物差不多，所以选这选那，并不是现代人的创造，而早在一千年以前就有了。而且这里要提一下，斗茶也是最早的茶道，斗也是一种表演，有阵式，有规则，现场气氛热烈而庄重。现在有人说日本人发明茶道，这至少是一种无知。

现在，中国茶大致可分六个基本大类：第一类，绿茶。采下的新鲜茶叶，不经过任何发酵，只经过大锅炒干即成，有的用手工翻炒，茶叶变成扁平、卷曲、针形等，整齐美观。绿茶的优点是，经过水冲泡后，茶叶还原成翠绿，形状漂亮，茶水清澈，保持了原来的色香味，著名的有龙井、碧螺春、毛峰等。花茶是绿茶在烘炒后用茉莉花或玫瑰花等鲜花窨制，使茶叶兼有花的香味。第二类是经过半发酵的乌龙茶。茶水清亮微黄，茶香特别浓郁，著名的有高山云雾茶、铁观音等。另外一类是经过发酵的红茶。红茶著名的有大红袍、祁门红茶等，可清饮，或加糖和牛奶。还有一类是近年颇为流行的普洱茶，属于黑茶，产于云南，经过发酵，做成茶饼或散茶。普洱茶不像其他茶叶，越新越好，它是越陈越香，所以它也变成了时尚的收藏品。此外，还有黄茶和白茶。

茶的文化

"青山个个伸头看，看我庵中吃苦茶"，这两句诗集中表现了饮茶的高雅意境。有一座清静寺庙，坐落在远离尘世的深山里，一个人正在悠闲地喝着茶，妙就妙在，他不说他一边喝着茶，一边看着青山，而说青山伸着头在看他喝茶。喝茶就是要有恬静心态，喝茶又能使人消除各种世俗杂念，增加闲情逸致。中国人在生活的各个方面都要追求和标榜清高，包括琴棋书画，无不如此，这两句诗说青山看着他喝茶，环境清冷，喝茶的人喝得心旷神怡，这正表现了一种喝茶的最高境界，这就是中国人的茶文化。

茶树对气候很敏感，严冬过去，大地回春，它就开始萌芽，春芽在清明以前采摘最好，一个芽包含三片嫩叶，采集后，用大锅杀青，人工翻炒，变成绿茶片。绿茶最好用80℃左右的水在玻璃杯中冲泡，碧绿的叶子好像得到生命还原，茶水清澈，散发出一股幽香。当茶泡好以后，先可以闻香味，欣赏茶的颜色，然后喝一小口，让茶水在舌尖停留，细细品味，叫做品茶。茶刚入口时，它味道清醇微苦，不久有了甜味，同时，茶的清香散布到整个口腔鼻腔，在把茶水慢慢咽下时，甘甜也随之沁人心脾，所以，会喝茶的人讲究一点一点地品茶，如果大口喝茶，就变成牛饮了。喝绿茶如此，喝好的乌龙茶也如此。

唐代出现了一部有名的论茶专著《茶经》，作者陆羽，他因此得到"茶圣"的称号。《茶经》是古代一部最完备的关于茶的产地、茶的种植，以及采茶、加工茶和喝茶的百科全书，书里专门提到了水对茶的重要作用，好茶必须用好水，好茶好水相得益彰，否则，水会破坏茶的色香味。陆羽游历大江南北，遍尝各地泉水，鉴定哪里的泉水最好，认为庐山谷帘泉"第一"。与陆羽同时代的刘伯刍则认为"天下第一泉"在镇江，"天下第二泉"在无锡。但现在，天下第二泉远比天下第一泉有名，这是因为近代无锡出了一位瞎子音乐家阿炳，他创作的一首二胡独奏曲《二泉映月》，曲调幽静婉转优美，蜚声全国，使其他江南丝竹相形见绌。不过，除了极个别嘴巴挑剔的人以外，第一泉的水和第二泉的水，是很难分上下的，倒是有的小

陆羽品茶图

133

说对茶水的描写更有味道，像《红楼梦》里妙玉泡茶招待宝钗、黛玉，用的水就非常特别：在冬天，她把梅花上的雪收集起来，装在盛器里，埋在地下十年方才拿出来。

关于中国的茶文化，还有几点必须提一提。首先是中国的茶馆，茶馆在南北朝时就有了，叫茶寮，寮意思是小屋子。后来茶馆慢慢多起来，到了元代明代，随着城市发展和市民阶层的出现，茶馆里请来艺人表演戏曲、说唱和讲故事等，来喝茶的顾客可以一边喝茶、吃糕点和硬壳果之类，一边欣赏表演，一坐下来就是几个钟头，茶馆实际上兼有了剧场的功能。这种茶馆兼剧场的形式，十分适应中国的社会经济条件和人们的生活习惯，所以它在全国城乡遍地开花，长期以来成为普通老百姓主要的休闲娱乐场所。其次，必须提到茶具，除了玻璃杯、瓷杯外，这里着重说一下紫砂壶。紫砂壶的产地是江苏宜兴，这里的土质特别好，烧出的紫砂器皿成紫红色，细腻有光泽。特别是历史造就了一批紫砂艺人，他们制作出来的紫砂壶造型高雅、古朴、精美，不同凡响，盖上盖子不漏水，碰一碰茶壶会发出金属般的声音。人们用紫砂壶喝茶，可以同时把玩欣赏茶壶的艺术造型，增加喝茶的情趣。茶文化最后要说一说茶道表演，这是在人多的时候，为活跃气氛和提高乐趣的一种集体喝茶形式，最早是在新茶上市的时候，一些喝茶爱好者聚集在一起，喝茶，议论茶，作为一种人际交流，打破了通常一个人形单影只地喝茶的习惯。后来，一些茶叶推销商就采用茶道表演来吸引顾客。

酒的传统

酒的起源有一个传说：原始人用果子酿酒，作为诱饵，放在森林里，猿和猴子看见了便来喝，一喝便纷纷醉倒，被人捉住。但另有一个说法：有一次原始人走进一个猿洞，发现有水果酿成的酒，于是也学会了酿酒。这些传说有个共同点，就是酿酒起源很早，是由果子发酵制成。史书记载酒的起源也有多种说法，有的说三皇五帝造酒，有的说尧造酒，还有人说一个叫杜康的人造酒，杜康是夏代第六个君主，至少，他是最早一个有名有姓的酿酒专家。后来，史料记载商代纣王"以酒为池，以肉为林，使男女裸，相逐其间"，这是说纣王叫一群男女裸体，躲在酒池肉林里捉迷藏，可见这场地也是够大的了。到唐代初年，唐军征服了新疆一个小国家，得到了葡萄酒和酿造葡萄酒的技术，从此内地也开始生产葡萄酒了。关于何时发明白酒，也有不同意见，有史书说是元代，但是考古学家出土了一个汉代青铜蒸馏器，认为汉代已经有白酒了，两种意见时间大相径庭，差距竟达一千年。

中国人造酒的用料用水和制作流程都很讲究，黄酒传统产地在浙江绍兴，过去当地有个习俗，一个家庭生下女婴，就要做一缸酒，埋在地下，等到女孩长大，在婚礼酒

《八仙醉酒》（年画）

席上拿出来招待宾客。葡萄酒的佳品多出产在北方，而白酒历来有所谓五大名酒，产自全国各地，目前，茅台酒和五粮液酒已成为驰名海内外的名酒。

酒的文化

人类各个民族各个社会对酒的生产和消费，有一定的共性，饮酒是人类生活的一部分，富人有富人的饮酒方法，穷人有穷人的饮酒方法，人多有人多的饮酒方法，人少有人少的饮酒方法，等等，那么，中国的酒文化有哪些自身的特点呢？

首先，中国历代文人，如果屈指一个一个数过来，大多对酒有特殊爱好，和酒有特殊关系，酒融入了他们的生活，支配了他们的行为，影响了他们的感情，这就是说，酒对提高文学家、艺术家和诗人们的创作欲望，激发他们的创作灵感，具有直接的不可代替的作用。数不清的被传诵千古的诗、词、文、赋，受到过酒的启发，得到过酒的灵感，许多内容直接描写酒，或与酒有关，试想，如果没有酒，这些诗、词、文、赋还能成为诗、词、文、赋吗？中国传统文学宝库会是个什么样子？这里随手拈来几个例子，像"对酒当歌，人生几何"，这是集会时的诗；"衔觞赋诗，以乐其志"，这是叙说个人志趣的诗；"两人对酌山花开，一杯一杯复一杯，我醉欲眠君且去，明朝有意抱琴来"，这是休闲的诗；"主称会面难，一举累十觞"，这是朋友久别重逢的诗；"劝君更尽一杯酒，西出阳关无故人"，这是朋友送别的诗，等等。

再有一点，中国人喜欢用酒营造热闹气氛，在婚庆喜事、纪念集会等宴席上，有了酒，气氛就热烈起来，中国人喝酒不是各喝各的，互不相干，而是集体地有交流

地喝，所谓喝酒行令，杯觥交错。行令也就是猜酒，猜错了要罚酒，像李商隐的诗句"隔座送钩春酒暖"，说的就是这情况，从整首诗看来，对方是朋友家的女主人，两人还隐隐约约有"心有灵犀一点通"的感受。后来，为了追求热闹，猜拳发展成为猜手指数，猜拳时，两人同时伸出几只手指，同时喊出一个数字，猜两个人的手指加起来是多少，输的人罚酒。上一篇曾经提到曹植诗"鸣俦啸匹侣"，显然是描写猜拳的热烈场面。直到今天，猜拳的传统在广大城乡还十分流行，每逢喜庆宴会，那些会喝酒爱热闹的人聚集在一起猜拳吆喝，人声鼎沸，输的人喝了三杯败下阵去，保持不败势头的人可以一路过关斩将。

最后附带说一下，中国历史上最壮观的饮酒场面：汉代大将军霍去病征讨匈奴打了胜仗，汉武帝送一百坛酒犒赏军队，皇帝本来是送酒给一些高级将领喝，但霍去病决定让全体士兵分享。士兵有十万人，怎样分享呢？他把一坛酒倒在一条泉水里，让一千个士兵来一起喝水，喝完了再倒一坛，再让一千个士兵喝。当时十万个人喝胜利酒，这样的场面可以说是：欢声震大地，雷鼓动山川。后来这条泉水被改名为酒泉，当地城市也改名为酒泉，它就是现在中国著名的卫星发射基地。

Chapter 14
Tea And Wine

T ea Tradition

China was a nation having the longest history of cultivating tea in the world, and Chinese people were also enthusiastic to drink tea. There was a saying began prevailing in Song Dynasty dated back 1,000 years ago: A household needs 7 stuffs when opening the door in the morning: firewood, rice, oil, salt, bean sauce, vinegar and tea. In the South & North Dynasties Period (420—581), people improved processing tea technique by leavening and drying tea leaves into lump tea, that made it much easier for people to store, transport and trade tea. Tea became an important commodity, and by then, some Turkish business men also began to traffic tea from China to Turkey, then to Europe through the Silk Road.

In Song Dynasty, there came out a tea-contest carnival that became a driving force to stir up Chinese tea culture. The carnival was sponsored by central government annually in the capital Kaifeng, Henan Provine, and attended by provincial delegations

A court tea banguet

from all over the country. The contest began with an exhibition fair, ensued by a tea-making performance, and then finally, an expert group appraised the tea qualities of each delegation, announced the winners list of competitors. Nowadays, someone alleged that Japanese initiated the tea-making performance, those people, at least, were lack of historical knowledge.

Chinese tea was now classified into three categories: green tea, wulong (yellow) tea and black tea. Green tea boasted its tea leaves' original color and flavor, its water appeared lovely green and transparent. The wulong tea has strong fragrance, its water was light yellow and transparent, because been shortly leavened. The black tea was usually sold on the international markets.

Tea Culture

Chinese tea lovers have a strong opinion on a special conception when drinking tea: a peaceful environment as well as a tranquil inner mind. They usually at first appreciated the water color, smelled the aroma, and then took a small sip of tea, left the water on the tongue, and let its fragrance spread in the mouth. Chinese tea enthusiasts usually sat alone on a silent scene, and calmed their mind down and drove away their day-to-day thinking through drinking tea. In Tang Dynasty (618—907), there was a tea sage Lu Yu wrote a book titled *Tea Bible*, famous for its integrated summing up the knowledge about tea cultivation, processing and classification. He also pointed out that the water was an important part for making tea. He had traveled around the south and north of Yangtze River, tasted the water of all rivers and springs, and finally granted a spring in Zhenjiang, Jiangsu Province the title as "Nation's Number 1 Spring", granted the another in Wuxi the title as "Nation's Number 2 Spring". But afterward, the Spring Two became much more popular than Spring One because of the appearance of a nationally acclaimed er-hu (string instrument) music *The Spring Two under Moonlight* created by a poor blind musician Ah Bing in early 1930s.

There were two more things important about Chinese tea culture: teahouse and teapot. Teahouse began to prevail in Yuan Dynasty (1260—1368), when more teahouses were built up in cities and towns, and the teahouse owners began to invite artists to perform folk operas and story-telling in the house. Customers could spend couple of hours enjoying recreation over sipping tea or

Porcelain teapot

eating some refreshments. As for teapot, the best teapot was produced in Yixing, Jiangsu Province, where provided two requirements for making pot: good mud material and skillful craftsmanship. The teapots made by the experienced craftsmen usually appeared gracefully-shaped, beautifully-colored. They would give out metallic sound when been gently stricken. So, the teapot was also of high artistic value.

Wine Tradition

The history of making wine in China could be dated back to pre-historical era. In late Shang Dynasty (1562—1066 BC) , the tyrant emperor Zhouwang was reportedly to build up a garden made of a wine pool and meat forest, and he ordered some naked young boys and girls playing the game of hide and seek in it.

Chinese people had a tradition of drinking yellow wine, a kind of wine unique in flavor made of rice. The star town of yellow wine was Shaoxing, Zhejiang Pravince, where there was a local custom passed down for generations, i.e., when a family gave birth to a girl baby, they would brew a big container of yellow wine, buried it under the ground. When the girl was of age, the family would take out the old-aged wine catering relatives and friends at the girl's wedding feast.

Good water was essential for making good wine. For hundreds of years, there were 8 name brands of white spirit produced in different provinces in China, and now "Maotai" and "Wuliangye" produced in Guizhou Province became up-and-coming in recent tens of years, and their market shares were keeping growing both in home and abroad.

Wine Culture

China had its own distinct feature of wine culture, as following:

Firstly, all the renowned men of letters, poets, calligraphers and painters in all dynasties were the huge thirst for wine. There were numerous stories and legends describing how they loved drinking wine. Wine always stimulated the men of letters or artists' creative impulse, and made their emotion sparkling with ingenuity and fantasy. In other sense, wine helped the men

A master checks wine's quality

of letters or artists achieve their glorious and classical masterpieces. People believe, if there was no wine, Chinese literature would actually become lusterless and insipid.

In addition, Chinese people liked having companions when drinking. They often played games. It's said, in Han Dynasty (206 BC—25 AD), Emperor Wudi had a concubine whose left hand always grasped tight, Wudi forced open her fist, and found there was a small jade hook in it. People began to play the game guessing from each other if the fist had a hook. If one made a good guess, the loser would be punished by drinking a cup of wine. Anytime the game began, the wine feast would become exciting and noisy. Afterward, the game was improved. The duelists stretched out their fists, showed some fingers, and at the same time shouting out a number that must equal to the sum of two fists' fingers. The game have still been a fashion prevailing in holiday get-togethers or happy ceremonies in cities and countryside. In joyous occasions, men find companions and play guessing fist games that always make the scene become heating and pompous.

There was a scene most pompous and spectacular in drinking wine history. In Han Dynasty, a military commander Huo Qiubing won a decisive war over Xiong Nu troops, and Emperor Wudi sent 100 jars of wine and bounteous food to reward the army. The wine was only enough for rewarding high rank generals, but Huo wanted to share it with all his hundred thousand troops. So, what he could do? He ordered to pour one jar of wine into a river, and let thousand troops to drink the water, and then pouring another jar of wine, and let another thousand troops to drink. A great scene then showed up: Cheers sounded like thunder, and beating drums quivered the mountains and rivers. Because of the event, the river had been renamed as the "Wine Spring", and a new city built up as a border fortress was also named "Wine Spring City" in west Gansu Province. Currently, the Wine Spring City (Jiuquan City) has become more popular and important than ever as it was the place for launching satellite in China.

服饰文化

第十五篇

服饰的发展演变

中国人数千年来一直称自己为礼仪之邦，因此，服饰名目之繁多、品类之复杂、形式之丰富，世界上任何其他民族都是无法比拟的，这也是中国服饰的最大特点。原始人的服饰这里省略不讲了。春秋战国时期，中国出现第一次文化高峰，人们开始重视衣饰，并且把衣饰和礼节挂起钩来。一般来说，读书人和有地位的人穿长衣，峨冠宽袍博袖，很神气的，而劳动人民穿劣质短衣裤，叫"褐"。那时候中原人和少数民族人的衣着最大区别是，中原人"束发右衽"，就是头发卷在头上，因为人们认为"身体发肤，受之父母，不敢毁伤"，是从来不剪头发的，衣服像现在的婴儿服，胸前两片重叠，用带子缚住，左边压右边叫右衽。而少数民族人则是"披发左衽"，就是头发披散，衣服右边压左边。到了东晋和南北朝时期，少数民族占领大半个中国，建立了政权，他们的统治阶层掀起学习汉文化的运动，改穿汉族服装，学习峨冠宽袍，而许多汉族人也反过来喜欢穿胡服，因为胡服紧身窄袖，下面穿靴子，便于骑马射箭。总之，这三百多年时间里，人们衣服的式样最乱，达到"乱穿衣"的地步。到了唐代，汉族人对少数民族的服装兴趣仍然不减，以穿胡服为时尚，连妇女们也爱穿胡服，戴胡帽。汉族人的女服本来很保守，而胡装比较开放自由，汉族妇女仿效胡服，把领子开得很低，有圆领、尖领、袒领等，唐代社会的审美观认为妇女以微胖为美，所以妇女们因此把肌肤露出来。

接下来几个朝代，宋代、明代是汉族政权，服饰基本上因袭唐代，元代是蒙古族政权，因为统治时间很短，他们的服饰对社会影响较少，清代是满族政权，又是中国最后一个封建王朝，统治时间也比较长，所以满族服装对近代中国的服饰影响很大，这一点人们可以从现在的舞台戏曲和电影里看出来，在有关明代的戏里，人们穿汉族服装，清代戏里，人们穿满族服装。

服饰的文化因素

一个民族的文化对服饰有很大影响，尤其在中国，下面分几方面来探究。

儒家思想的影响　儒家思想突出"礼"，所以中国人穿衣服的各种规矩特别多，各类人，各类场合，穿什么衣服都有规定，做官的有官服、便服、祭服、礼服，地主穿绅士服，读书人穿士服，考中秀才、举人以后可以穿秀才服、举人服，普通百姓穿粗服，连衣服颜色都有规定，不能逾越，这点在后面戏曲服装一节里还要谈到。儒家歧视妇女，要妇女守女德，女服都是长袖长裤长裙，不能露出肌肤（要笑不露齿，衣不露肤），这里有一个故事：孟子有一次偶然到妻子住的里屋去，当时正是大热天，见妻子只穿短衫短裙，他一看就大发脾气，认为她不守妇道，坚持要写休书把妻子退回娘家去（几千年来，男人只要写一张字据，就可以把妻子"休"掉）。还好这时候孟母出来讲公道话说，这么热天，你不打招呼进来，她一个人穿短衣短裙不可以吗？于是孟子无话可说。

服装文化的另一个重要表现，就是体现严格的等级制，这里特别来讲一讲帽子。几千年来，中国人一般都要戴帽子，劳动人民把头发卷成发髻，再裹上一块布就行了，知识分子和有身份的人，在发髻上面还要戴帽，十六岁成年要举行戴冠仪式，所以"年方弱冠"就是指刚戴上帽子的年轻人。帽子不是为了装饰和好看，主要是体现身份和地位，尤其是官帽。明代的官帽，里面是用铁丝绕成的帽架，外面裹一层黑色的纱，叫"乌纱帽"，这样的帽子戴在头上肯定一点也不舒服，但人人争着要戴。乌纱帽左右两边伸出两条像翅膀一样的东西，翅膀的长短、大小、形状，代表官职的高低，所以历来在民间，乌纱帽就成了官位的代名词，说一个人"戴上乌纱帽"，就是做官了，说"丢

唐朝贵妇人服饰

了乌纱帽"，就是被免官了，免官也叫"免冠"，官员退休回家叫"挂冠归田"。清代官员的帽子叫顶戴，也叫顶戴花翎，用顶戴花翎的形状和颜色来区分官位高低。所以历史上冠和官成了同一个含义，诗人杜甫有两句诗"冠盖满天下，斯人独憔悴"，感叹京城里有这么多人做官，自己却在京城悲惨旅居三十年，连一个官职也没捞到。

戏曲服装

今天的人们要想对传统服饰有一个具体形象的概念，不妨去看一些传统的戏曲，舞台上出现的各类人物，他们从头到脚的衣饰，除了装饰部分，例如皇冠、凤冠上的珠翠不是真珠翠，武将身上的铁甲不是真铁甲外，基本上保持了原来的样式、色彩和风貌。也许有人怀疑，舞台上许多人物的帽子式样很夸张，衣服大红大绿，很戏剧化，当时的真实生活会是这样的吗？回答是肯定的。传统的衣服特别讲究颜色，它表现不同的身份、地位，不能乱来，像黄色是皇帝专用的，皇帝的衣服也叫黄袍，因为黄色代表土和大地，谁要穿黄色衣服，就要被定为谋反罪，要被杀头。宰相以下到知府各级官员穿红色，县令穿青色，再下面的官吏和平民穿绿色和杂色，还有新科状元穿红色，新郎穿红色。另外，在官服的胸前有一块方形图案，图案里绣的是什么，这也很重要，皇帝黄袍绣的是龙，宰相服绣鹤，部长、省长级的绣锦

戏曲服装

143

鸡，再下面依次是绣孔雀、大雁、鹭鸶等，武将系列中，最高一级将领绣狮子，大将绣老虎，再下面依次是绣豹、熊、犀牛等。

戏曲服装里有地位妇女的帽子形状特别夸张，现实生活确实也是这样，举一个例子：明代的皇后凤冠，先用竹子编成框架，周围饰以黄金和珠翠，上面一共有九条翡翠龙，四只黄金凤，当中一条龙，口里衔一颗大珍珠，其余的龙和凤都衔小珍珠，龙凤周围还装饰翡翠云片40片，大珠花12枝，小珠花12枝，大珠花上各有牡丹花两朵，等等。这些东西加起来，这顶凤冠分量是够重的了。其实不但皇后和皇妃，其他受过封号的妇女，所谓命妇，戴的帽子也都差不多，只是龙和凤换成别的鸟，许多富贵人家不受条令限制，私自设计各式各样帽子，人们在戏曲舞台上常常看到富贵人家的千金小姐，头上也戴着很大很漂亮的帽子，满头黄金珠翠，可见这种式样夸张的妇女帽子，当时在社会上是并不罕见的。

接下来要说一说服装上的绣花。现代服装的色彩是印花机印出来，以前主要靠绣花。古代中国社会男耕女织，家家户户妇女自己纺纱织布，绣花也是妇女的一门基本手艺，所以衣服上绣花很普及，是中国服装的另一个重要特色。上面已说过帝王将相衣服上绣龙凤鸟兽，其他人们的衣服，也按性别、男女老幼、身份和社会地位，绣上各种图案，有装饰性的，象征吉祥的，象征长寿的，不一而足。其中，妇女服饰的绣花特别讲究，衣服上绣花，是绣衣，裙子上绣花，是绣花裙，鞋子上绣花，是绣花鞋，手绢上绣花，是绣罗帕，小包上绣花，是绣荷包，等等。唐代妇女的裙子很有特点，很长很宽大，除了绣花裙以外，还流行一种石榴裙，每到春天石榴花开，家家户户采摘或购买石榴花染裙子，裙子呈深红色。诗人白居易有"血色罗裙翻酒污"的诗句，后来又出现

老月份牌上的旗袍

"拜倒在石榴裙下"的成语，是说一个男人拜倒在一个女子脚下。关于绣花裙，史书上记载制作最神奇的一条裙子，是中唐时代一位公主的"百鸟裙"，巧匠们采集百鸟的羽毛，综合用纺、织、绣等方法，做成的裙子非常特别，白天看是一种颜色，灯光下看又是一种颜色，从左边看是一种颜色，从右边看又是一种颜色，而且裙子上面还有百鸟的栩栩如生的形象。这样的手艺，用平常的"巧夺天工"四字去形容，已经显得不够有光彩了。

唐 装

唐装，是近年来出现的一个新名词，意思是中国传统式服装，因为在其他国家许多中国人聚居的地区，都叫"唐人街"、"唐人区"，用唐字代表中国，易于为一般外国人所接受。其实，唐代距今已经一千三四百年，唐装并不是真正唐代人穿的服装，今天的所谓唐装，主要是满族人的服装样式。满族政权清王朝是中国最后一个封建王朝，它统治中国两百多年，时间比较长，所以，唐、宋、明朝代的原来汉人的服饰已经被取代。满族装的便装，男式有长袍短衣之分，长袍的衣扣开在右边，短衣衣扣开在胸前，基本上就是今天的唐装式样。女式服装叫旗袍，旗也是满族的意思，

时装仕女图（月份牌）

旗袍的特点是式样简单朴素，能够显示女性体态的曲线美。

清政府被推翻后，为了革除清王朝的皇袍官服，孙中山创造性地设计了一种"中山装"，采用西式服装裁剪法，领口用小领子，胸前有四个口袋，口袋都有扣子。中山装比较实用大方，所以在新中国成立之后，它实际上成了中国的国服。现在的中国

社会服装呈现多样化，许多人节日里穿上唐装，别具风采。

　　中国有56个民族，每个民族都有自己的民族服装，像藏族、蒙古族、朝鲜族等，民族服装都很有特色，苗族、壮族、彝族等许多民族服装，不但花花绿绿，而且人们的头上手上都戴满装饰品。

Chapter 15

Dressing

Dressing Tradition

China has boasted of its long tradition of advocating etiquette ceremonies, and therefore Chinese dressing system embraced a good assortment of styles and designs and made it differ from any other nation's dressing tradition in the world. Dressing included clothing and personal adornment. In Spring & Autumn Period (770—476 BC), when China saw the first cultural upsurge, people began to put dressing to connect with etiquette. Officials and the people with high social status attired high hat and long and broad robe, for the sake of expressing their elegant and noble atmosphere, while the populace were mostly poorly dressed. Afterward, the invasion of ethnic minorities brought about great changes of Chinese dressing culture. In South & North Dynasties (420 AD—581), when five most powerful ethnic minorities occupied broad territory of north China, their rulers began to learn and adopt Han majority's culture, including changing their original attire tradition. But vise versa, Han people at the time also warmly accepted ethnic minorities' clothing, because it was body-hugging, convenient for riding horses and shooting arrows. In Tang Dynasty, the ethnic minorities' dressing continued to find favor with Han majority people. (see chapter 4) Song and Ming dynasties continued Tang's clothing tradition. But Qing Dynasty was an ethnic Manchu government, and because Qing was the last imperial dynasty in Chinese history, and also its ruling lasted for more than 2 hundred years, ethnic Manchu's dressing has actually given a significant impact to China's modern clothing trend.

Dressing Culture

As a nation's culture would bring about a weighty influence to its dressing custom, it was especially true in China. At first, people saw the influence imposed on by Confucius doctrine. Confucius advocated etiquette, causing Chinese clothing to demonstrate strict stereotyped conventions, i. e., every person in different social status wore their different type of clothes: officials' clothes (also including official clothes, plain clothes, ceremonial

Emperor's dragon robe of Qing Dyrasty

clothes and worshipping clothes), landlord clothes, intellectual's clothes (including high and low) and common people clothes. Confucius doctrine especially discriminated against women, wanting women to abide so-called "women moral codes", banning women to show teeth when smiling and show skin when put on clothes. As a result, women had to dress the clothes with long sleeves and long skirts for the sake of covering their skin. Chinese dressing also reflected strict social status system (hierarchy), especially the hat, which always indicated their identities. There was a kind of hat named "black-gauzed hat" as it was made of a steel-wired skeleton been covered with a coat of black gauze. It seemed never to make people comfortable when having put it on, but people always scrambled to want it, because it indicated an official post. There were two things something like wings stretched out from both sides of the hat, and the pattern and size of the wings were the indications of the official level. And actually, the "black-gauzed hat" became the replacement word of "official". It was very popular, when people said "someone has put on a black-gauzed hat", that meant someone has become an official. If said "someone lost his black-gauzed hat", that meant someone was removed from his post. So, sometimes the two words "hat" and "official post" sounded the same meaning. When people said "hanging up one's hat and back farming", that meant an official retired and back to his home in countryside. The official hat style in Qing Dynasty was differed from that in Ming. The ethnic minority Qing's official hats were divided the official levels by using different colors of peacock's feathers.

Theatrical Costume

People, who currently wanted to obtain a concept about Chinese traditional clothing, could go to the theater to watch a traditional opera or watch opera programs on TV. The costume from head to foot all characters wore on the stage were the replica in old dynasties, and of course, the precious pearls on the emperor's hat or steel helmet and armor worn by military officers were forgeries. Some people might be suspicious whether the colors and styles of the costume were truly lifelike, because they looked so exaggerated or dramatized. But the answer was positive. Taking the costume color for example, in the real life of old dynasties, people always took serious on their clothes color. The clothes color for emperor was fixed to yellow, as the color yellow represented the soil or land. So, anyone would be regarded to usurp the throne and be executed if he dared to wear yellow clothes. Besides, high officials wore in red, county governors wore in blue, and common people only wore parti-colored clothes. There was also a square of decorating area in the chest of clothes embroidered with different birds and animals. The emperor's clothes were embroidered with dragons, civil officials' clothes were embroidered with different birds, and military officers' clothes were embroidered with different animals. In addition, women' hat was also especially exaggeratedly-shaped in stage. It's said, the queen's hat in Ming Dynasty was decorated with 9 dragons and 4 phoenixes made of gold and jadeite, and each of them held a pearl in its mouth, as well as been surrounded with jadeite clouds and flowers. The women in other families of wealth and rank wore the hat looked something the same, and the only difference was they used other birds instead of dragons and phoenixes.

Besides, the embroidery was also a spotlight of Chinese dressing culture. China was a nation of "men plough and women weave", and every women learned embroidering skill when they were young, and were good in embroidery when they grew up. The tradition passed down generation by generation. For a long history, all walks of life except the poor, wore embroidered clothes with patterns of varied kinds of birds and flowers, or symbols of auspice and longevity, in accordance with their age, sex, wealth condition and social status. Embroidered clothes for women became so vogue, that women usually put on embroidered clothes, embroidered skirts, embroidered shoes, used embroidered handkerchiefs and embroidered handy bags.

Tang Style Fashion

"Tang style fashion" was a new word appeared only in recent twenty years, meaning "Chinese traditional clothes". It was actually not a fashion prevailed among the people in Tang Dynasty dated back 14 hundred years ago, and the word "Tang fashion" was only considered to be acceptable for foreigners, as the words "Chinese" and "Tang" sounded the same meaning in most foreign countries. (They call "Chinese Town" as "Tang-People Town", for example) The current so-called Tang style

Emperor Taizong of Tang Dynasty

149

fashion was actually a fashion of ethnic Manchu of Qing Dynasty (Manchu woman's fashion was called cheongsam). Because Qing had ruled China for more than 250 years, so, the ethnic Manchu's clothing had replaced Han majority's clothing in Ming Dynasty. Currently the clothing habits of Chinese people become modernized and diversified, they usually put on Tang style fashion to show their easy manner in holidays or festivals. In China, there are many ethnic minorities' people having their own traditional attires, with which they especially dress up themselves in various festive occasions.

手工艺品

　　中国手工艺品的品类浩繁，大多历史悠久，工艺技术精湛，具有明显的民族特色，中国手工艺品是中国民族文化中的一串璀璨明珠。这篇短文里只能很简单扼要地叙述一下。

青铜器

　　青铜器是中国先民发出的最早的智慧光芒。青铜器在夏代晚期就有了，到商代进入繁荣期，一直延续到春秋战国，历时一千多年（公元前1500—220年），它主要有礼器"鼎"和乐器"钟"两大类，鼎和钟上都刻有文字，记载祭祀活动或一段特殊历史。目前最大、最珍贵的青铜器，是在河南安阳出土的商代后期的一只大方鼎，高133厘米，长110厘米，宽78厘米，重达875公斤，鼎的四周有象征吉祥的云纹图案，当中是一只又像鳄鱼又像蛇的怪兽，凸显狰狞、神秘、威严的气氛，鼎上刻有"司母戊"三个字，说明这只鼎是主人用来祭祀他母亲的祭具。钟是打击乐器，1978年在湖北出土一套战国初期编钟，共有65枚，打击时按大小厚薄发出不同声音，居然和现在国际通用C大调e的音阶相同，包含五个八度。钟和鼎上刻的文字叫钟鼎

司母戊大方鼎

文，是甲骨文以后，比篆字早的一种文字。除了钟和鼎，比较小的青铜器还有兵器、餐具和其他各种日常用具，说明青铜器在当时贵族中已经十分流行。

青铜器是利用铜和锡浇铸出来的合金，现在辽宁、湖南、湖北三省都发现了古代开采和冶炼铜矿的遗址，先民已经解决了耐火材料、熔化金属和用模子浇铸的技术，而且还对青铜器毛坯进行抛光、雕刻和涂金。古代青铜器作为中国早期的一种手工艺，它造型精致、大方美观，而且具有很高的科技含量，它们现在陈列在博物馆里，成为中国古代文明的一个亮点。

陶器和瓷器

中国在2500年前的商周墓穴中就发现了瓷器。中国很早就有高度的瓷器文明，这是普世公认的，在英语中，china即瓷器的意思。在瓷器出现以前，人们在生活中使用陶器，而陶器在7000年前就有了。春秋时期出现了陶俑，那时候王公贵族（奴隶主）死了，流行用活人陪葬，对这一惨绝人寰的做法，孔子用最激烈语言提出控诉，说"始作俑者，其无后乎"，就是说，带头用活人陪葬的人，一定要断子绝孙（现在有人喜欢用始作俑者这个成语，注意这是骂人话）。后来人们开始改变习惯，慢慢用陶

马家窑彩陶

俑来代替活人了。在秦始皇陵地下发现的兵马俑，是秦代陶塑艺术的奇迹，后来在唐代又发明了唐三彩，就是用黄、绿、白三色釉彩涂在陶器外面，一般都是马、骆驼和各种人物俑等，它们当时也是用来陪葬的。唐代以后陶器工艺逐渐衰落，到现在只有紫砂壶和一些传统人物雕塑流传下来。

陶器衰落过程也就是瓷器加速发展的过程，瓷器发展大概可分三个阶段：最初的瓷器以青瓷为主，表面青绿晶莹，质地细密，碰触会发出金属声。唐宋时期，瓷窑大量发展，官窑和民窑相

互竞争，各有优势，其中以浙江的龙泉窑和河南的均窑制造的青瓷为最珍贵，同时北方一些瓷窑烧出白色瓷器，形成南青北白的格局。第二阶段，在唐末出现了青花瓷，它打破了瓷器的单一颜色，而是以白为底色，上面描上青（深蓝）色花纹，青花瓷器青白相间，显得高雅、稳重、大方，一下提高了瓷器的品位和气质。元代、明代海运兴起，中国早期销往中东和欧洲的蜚声海外的"明瓷"，绝大多数都是青花瓷器。到了第三阶段，即明代中后期，青花瓷进一步向彩瓷发展，就是在青花基础上，加上了五彩颜色，在瓷器上描绘人物、花卉、禽鸟等内容，彩色釉还促进了装饰性品种，像造型各异的大型瓷瓶瓷缸的发展，到后来又出现单釉色多釉色装饰瓷瓶，争奇斗艳。这里要补充说明一点的是，这些釉的斑斓色彩，在瓷器没有加温前是没有颜色的，随着窑里升温，到1000℃，到1300℃，釉的不同颜色，才会一个层面一个层面地显示出来。中国的瓷器，到了清代初期和中期，它们的制作工艺和艺术性都达到了高峰。

今天，江西的景德镇被称为中国的瓷都，经过千百年的优胜劣汰，景德镇脱颖而出，成为引领全国瓷器产业的最大基地，这里生产规模大，人才优势集中，除了继承传统以外，在技术和工艺上也不断有所创新，中国的瓷器手工艺品还在继续发展中。

玉雕和木雕

中国的雕刻没有走西方雕刻艺术的道路，早在南北朝到隋唐时代，随着佛教的传入，兴起一股雕塑佛像的高潮，而雕塑的理念也和其他艺术一样，是写意的，追求抽象的造型美，这一时期流传下来的雕刻群，有著名的山西云冈石窟和河南的龙门石窟等，在岩石上雕刻的佛像造型高雅，表情安详，雕刻线条优美流畅，艺术性达到极高水平。此后，中国的雕塑没有作为一门专门艺术继续发展，只是皇帝和王公贵族死后，在他们陵墓的甬道两旁，摆上一些石人石马，还有，在富贵大户人家的家门口，往往有一对石狮子守门等。不过与此同时，雕塑却从另一个方向迅速发展起来，演变成接近人们日常生活的雕刻手工艺。中国的雕刻工艺也是五花八门，金属、玉石、竹木、漆器、象牙、砚台、印章、贝壳、树根，什么都雕，连在一粒米上也能雕出一首诗，几十个字，用放大镜可以清晰看到，这叫微雕。下面着重说一说玉雕和木雕。

玉雕 或叫玉石雕刻，是历史最悠久的一种手工艺。玉和石是个笼统的概念，好或坏标准说不清，但质量等级有天壤之别，一般粗糙的玉石也是玉，而一块小的翡翠

云冈石窟佛像

可以价值连城，所以有一个传统的说法：金子有价玉无价。古代人们相信玉可以避邪，有钱的人往往把雕刻精致的玉坠子、玉挂件带在身边，男人带的叫玉珂，女人带的叫环佩。近代以来，由于中国可供雕刻的玉石产量丰富，玉雕品被用于室内摆饰，受到人们的欢迎，因此市场兴旺，艺人们常常利用玉石的自然色泽和纹路来设计内容，有的利用得十分巧妙，这就大大提高了作品的品位，如某块玉石上有天然的紫红、白和翠绿颜色，艺人把紫色雕刻成一串葡萄，白色刻成盛器，最巧妙的是把一小块翠绿色刻成一只可爱的叫蝈蝈，整个作品就立刻变得生机盎然了。

木雕 中国一门重要的传统手工艺，长期来和人民生活极其密切。现在，当人们走进一个古建筑旅游点或民居博物馆，发现家具古色古香，所有的木制家具上都有精致雕刻，床的正面上上下下，都有浮雕或镂雕，内容大多是蝙蝠、吉祥鸟和奇花异草，图案复杂，手工精细，讲究的还镶金包银。其他的家具，像大柜、木箱、凳子，也是刻满花纹。这里还要特别提一样东西"屏风"，屏风摆设在屋子里，与其说是日用品，还不如说是艺术品，它一般用深色底漆，画面像中国画，包括人物、山水、花鸟，但是，这些形象都是利用玉石、珊瑚、贝壳、琥珀等天然颜色材料，雕刻好，一部分一部分镶嵌合成的，所以特别显得雍容华贵。古建筑的民居和亭台楼阁也一样，屋檐门窗都雕有花纹，主题大多是多子多福、松鹤长寿、财神献宝，以及象征吉祥的各种禽鸟花卉等。建筑物有了雕刻，不但看上去赏心悦目，而且有了文化和艺术的深度。到了近代，随着建筑理念的改变，木雕用于房屋装饰已不多见，传统的木雕手工艺向着旅游产业方向靠拢。

在现在的旅游景点，玉雕和木雕纪念品琳琅满目，有大有小，玉质木质有好有次，雕刻技艺各不相同，内容也包罗万象，凡是各种人物、龙凤蛇龟，十二生肖、飞禽走兽，应有尽有，它们成了市场上十分畅销的手工艺品。

丝绸和刺绣

刺绣是在丝绸织品上刺上各种花纹，也是中国历史悠久的一门独特手工艺。丝绸据说是史前时代黄帝的妻子嫘祖发明的，到了三千多年前的商周时代，人们已经能够造出质量相当高的丝绸，并且会在丝绸上染色。到了秦汉，长江以北养蚕缫丝已十分普遍，汉代开辟了丝绸之路以后，丝绸被骆驼队运往西方，引起轰动，那里丝绸的价格和黄金相等，有一次罗马帝国的凯撒大帝穿着一件丝绸长袍到剧场看戏，周围的人看了都啧啧称奇。在海外贸易中，千百年来中国丝绸一直负有盛名，成为中国的骄傲。

刺绣这一门手工艺，几乎是同丝绸生产同步发展的，上面说到，在商周时代，人们已经在丝绸上染色，但染色的效果是单色的，所以在这同时出现了刺绣，单色的丝绸经过五色彩线绣上各种图案形象，使它焕发光彩，艺术审美价值大大提高了。秦汉时代，刺绣逐渐普及，当时山东一带的老百姓世世代代刺绣，没有一个女子不会，河南一带的老百姓家家户户织绸缎，没有一个女子的手不巧，这是由于"日见之，日为之，手狎也"（天天看，天天做，手艺熟练了）。在著名的西汉马王堆一号出土文物里，文字记载刺绣的内容，有"信期绣"、"乘云绣"和"长寿绣"等，可见刺绣的手法变化已经很多了。历史上，中国的女子一般是不念书的，自小就在家里学"女红"，刺绣也自然是一门必修课，当时人们穿绣花衣服，女人还穿绣花鞋，在屋子里，人们用的被头是绣花被，蚊帐是绣花帐，枕头是绣花枕头，等等，所以，刺绣是数千年来和人们生活最密切、人们参与最广泛的一种传统手工艺。

古代丝绸织锦

到了近代，随着现代

印花和机器绣花行业的兴起，旧的手工刺绣快速衰落，不过，中国的刺绣，作为一门历史悠久的手工艺，它的精湛技艺被保留继承下来，转化成为一种专职手工工艺，刺绣作品成为一种高雅的装饰艺术，供人们观赏收藏。现在，中国的传统手工刺绣按风格不同，可分为苏绣（江苏）、蜀绣（四川）、粤绣（广东）和湘绣（湖南）四大派系。苏绣的特点是，作品精细，色彩和谐淡雅，题材以小动物、花卉、鱼虾为主；蜀绣的特点是，构图简练明快，针法严谨，内容以彩蝶、鲤鱼和熊猫等为主；粤绣的特点是，常在彩色线里加金银丝，绣品富丽堂皇，题材多是龙、凤、孔雀等，还有美轮美奂的戏剧服装；湘绣的内容和风格向中国画靠拢，常常以中国画为底，绣出山水云雾、亭台楼阁、飞禽走兽，尤其是狮子老虎一类猛兽，形象十分传神。

其 他

中国传统手工艺品还有很多，有些古老的手艺，像皮影戏等，已经面临失传，这里只能简单地提几种，不免挂一漏万。

剪纸　每当新年来到，许多人都有在家里柜子上或墙上贴红色剪纸的习惯，剪纸有的用剪刀剪，有的用刀刻，把一张红纸剪成复杂图案，内容一般都是表示祝福的文字，以及象征吉祥的喜鹊、鲤鱼、花草等。

面人　艺人先准备好染上各种颜色的面团，用几分钟时间，就可以把面团捏成人的头、身体、四肢，拼成一个小孩子或戏曲人物，逗人喜爱。

灯彩　艺人用细竹丝扎成灯的骨架，外面糊上透明纸和装饰纸，做成形态各异的花灯，有龙凤灯、孔雀灯、麒麟灯、荷花灯等，有人还利用热气上升的原理，把图案画在灯上，会转动，叫走马灯。

风筝　中国人放风筝已有悠久历史，现在在公园门口卖的风筝很粗糙，但也有不少用传统工艺制作的很精致的风筝。每到风筝节，各种大大小小风筝在沙滩上放飞，蔚为壮观。

Chapter 16

Handicrafts

Bronze Ware

Bronze ware was a symbol of Chinese early ancestors' wisdom and early civilization. There existed a Bronze Ware Era in Chinese history from Shang Dynasty (1562—1066 BC) to the Warring States Period (475—221 BC) lasted for 1,200 years. The bronze ware mainly included two categories: Ding (incense burner for worshiping ritual) and Zhong (percussion instrument). The biggest and most precious ding been discovered up-to-date was the one named "Shang Dynasty's Square Ding" unearthed from Anyang County, Henan Province. The ding measured 133 cm tall and weighted as heavy as 875 kg, with excellent modeling and superb workmanship: There was a strange animal something like a crocodile, something like a snake, staying at the center, assuming an atmosphere of prestige and mystery and surrounded by many pieces of auspice clouds. There also carved with three big early style characters on it, making clear that with this incense burner the owner played worship to his passed-away mother. In 1978, archaeologists unearthed a zhong series instrument from a tom of the late Warring States Period in Hubei Province. The zhong included 65 bronze pieces, each giving out different tone in accordance with their different size and thickness. The instrument stroke people as much, because it played pitch scale of music conforming perfectly with that of modern international standard. More, the instrument could play five sectors of eight degree sounds. The early style characters carved on the ding and zhong were called "zhong and ding letters", that was a kind of special letters in the developing process shortly after the inscriptions on shells and bones. Besides of ding and zhong, archaeologists also unearthed a variety of small bronze wares, such as swards, cooking utensils and other wares for day-to-day use, showing that during the time the bronze wares were not rare to be seen in aristocrat families.

Pottery And Porcelain

Chinese ancestors invented pottery 7,000 years ago, and archaeologists discovered a lot of various pottery dishes and jars in the ruins of the New Stone Era all around the

A colored porcelain bowl

country. In the Spring & Autumn period, people began to make pottery figurines been buried into the tomb to be the companions of the dead. The technology seemed quickly improved, and the terra-cotta warriors and horses in Emperor Shihuang tomb of Qin Dynasty (221—206 BC)discovered some 40 years ago were regarded as one of the greatest treasuries and ancient scientific wonders in the world.

China boasted of an early porcelain civilization, as the word "China" was originally meant porcelain. Archaeologists found the earliest porcelain utensils in Shang tombs dated back some 3,000 years ago. At the beginning, the porcelain utensils were mostly simply green-colored. In late Tang Dynasty, there came forth "blue decorative pattern" porcelain. The jade-white porcelain painted with dark-blue decorative pattern appeared a special bearing of elegance and refinement. In Yuan Dynasty, the boom of sea transportation prompted the development of international trade industry, and a large amount of China's porcelain products were exported to outside world. China's porcelain won a special prestigious name as "Ming Porcelain". In fact, the Ming porcelain products were mostly belonged to the blue decorative pattern porcelain. In mid and late Ming Dynasty, there came up colored decorative pattern porcelain that further increased the assortments and enhanced the artistic value of the porcelain products.

In recent tens of years, Jingdezhen Town of north Jiangxi Province became the star town of porcelain, where embraced all favorable conditions of traditional manufacturing technology and elite talents. The China's modern porcelain base now continues to assure the high level of porcelain production, and make new breakthrough of outputs featuring new styles and designs.

Jade And Wood Carving

Chinese sculpture artists took a road differed from what European artists did. Shortly after Buddhism spread in, Shui and Tang dynasties saw a thriving of carving Buddhist statues out of stone, and the representative sculpture works in the period were the Buddha groups in Yungang Grotto in Shanxi Province and Longmen Grotto in Henan Province. After that, Chinese sculpture artists gradually turned their attentions to carving handicrafts, including carving jade, wood, bamboo, lacquer ware, ivory, ink stone, chop, wood-root and shell.

China's jade-carving had a century-aged tradition. The value of jade-carving product

A scene of Longmen Grotto

was usually greatly diversified. A piece of common jade was not valued, but a small grain of emerald would be worth several cities. Craftsmen cleverly applied jade natural colors to carve different articles. They carved a white-and-green jade into a Chinese cabbage, and got a natural point of purple carved into a mantis. This kind of rare art treasure would become a collective in museums. At the same time, a lot of mid and low level jade-carving products were sold brisk in markets, as currently Chinese people like to buy jade or stone carving handicrafts to decorate their houses.

Wood carving had also a long tradition in China. When travelers visited age-old architectures in villages or residences, they could at first see wood carving decorations on eaves, doors, windows or even on different furniture that delight their eyes. In addition, there was a special furnishing attraction "pingfeng" meaning "screen". The pictures on the screen were something like Chinese traditional paintings, and the carved images in the picture such as birds, animals, flowers, trees, houses and human beings were all made of colors of natural jade, shell, coral and agate. Craftsmen at first carved them in parts, and then put them together. So pingfeng was a kind of indoor decoration with a special bearing of beauty and dignity. Though in modern buildings, people no longer used the traditional wood carving to decorate their doors, windows or furniture, the craft has played an important role in tourism industry, as travelers could find a wide range of lovely wood carving souvenirs displayed in rows of stalls in hot tourist spots.

Silk And Embroidery

The history of making silk could be dated back 5,000 years ago in China, as a legend described how Emperor Huangdi's wife Leizu instructed people to breed silk worms. In Zhou Dynasty dated back 3,000 years ago, people began to make quality silk, and dyed silk with different colors as well. In Han Dynasty, after the Silk Road was put to open, Chinese silk was trafficked to Mid Asia, Persian Gulf and Europe. It's said, The Kaiser The Great of Roman Empire once showed up at a party wearing a silk robe so rare that all the participants cast surprising eyes on him. In China, embroidery was also a time-honored household handicraft popularly prevailed both in towns and countryside. Historians recorded that every household weaved silk and every women did a good job in Henan Province, and every generation practiced embroidery and every women showed their skillfulness in Shandong Province. For thousands of years, people not

only wore clothes embroidered with various colorful patterns, but also used embroidered curtains, embroidered quilts and pillows in their day-to-day life. (see chapter 15) Currently, embroidery has become a traditional handicraft been inherited and carried on by professional embroidered experts and institutions, and the embroidered articles become a kind of mid and high level of art works finding favors among people both in home and abroad.

A big lying Buddha carved out of stone

阿房宫和秦始皇皇陵

　　中国建筑作为一种民族文化开始于春秋战国时代，那时诸侯国纷纷建立自己的都城，城市形成规模，建筑的屋顶已经采用木栋梁，上面铺瓦盖，用木柱承重，砖头砌墙，注重屋型美观。秦灭六国统一中国后，建造了阿房宫，这是一个历史标志性建筑。秦掳掠了六国财富珍宝，拥有全国人力，视人民如草芥，尤其是战俘百万，驱使如牲口，当时有历史性的三大工程同时开工，一是阿房宫，二是秦始皇皇陵，三是万里长城，各投入战俘数十万人。阿房宫体现君临天下，傲视万世的气

兵马俑

派，它位于今陕西省西安市以西，是一个绵延十五里的建筑群，唐代杜牧写了一篇有名的《阿房宫赋》，这样描述："覆压三百余里，隔离天日，两川溶溶，流入宫墙，五步一楼，十步一阁，各抱地势，钩心斗角。"还形容说："明星荧荧，开镜妆也，绿云扰扰，梳晓鬟也，渭流涨腻，弃脂水也（形容宫女早上梳头化妆）。"文章接着说许多宫女化妆等待皇帝，三十六年不曾见得一面。据文史说，阿房宫被楚霸王项羽放了一把火烧掉，大火烧了三天三夜不灭。文学作品的描写可能会有夸张，有的传说也可能不完全准确，例如，现在有些历史学家认为，阿房宫工程没有完工，秦始皇就死了，他儿子秦二世继续造，不久就天下大乱，秦代就覆亡了。还有，考古学家在阿房宫原址地下反复检测，没有发现灰烬和大火焚烧过的痕迹。但无论如何，阿房宫确实存在过，汉代和唐代历史学家和文学家的记述，还是值得后人尊重和参考的。

人们从阿房宫想到秦始皇皇陵，对于秦始皇皇陵大家没有争议了，它是个世界级的建筑奇迹。古代人相信人死后到阴府，阴府也是一个群体社会，和人世间一样，所以，帝王将相们都重视他们的陵墓建设，豪华精致，中国的陵墓文化是建筑文化的一个重要组成部分，正像埃及的金字塔是埃及古文化的珍珠一样，而中国墓葬更注意等级礼仪，仿生活化，以及死者要带走大量陪葬物，什么珍贵，就带走什么。秦始皇自从十三岁当诸侯王起，就开始为自己造坟墓，"刑徒七十万，起土骊山隈"，到他死，造了四十三年还没有完全造好。考古学家已经用先进仪器探明秦始皇皇陵的规模，因为现代的科技还无法保护出土的文物，所以陵墓还等待将来有一天开挖，到那时候，它的地下神秘面貌才会大白于天下。由于四十多年前当地农民无意中发现一些陶瓦碎片，一个庞大的兵马俑坑被发现，后来被命名为兵马俑一号坑，当时这一个发现立刻轰动全国，震惊世界。考古专家说，这个兵马俑坑只是秦始皇皇陵的冰山一角。除了秦始皇皇陵，中国历代帝王将相的陵墓不止几十个、几百个，而是成千上万，陵墓文化的价值远远超出建筑文化本身，它保存了大量在地面上难以保存和根本无法保存的古代文物，古代许多不解之谜，人们已经或正在通过墓葬里的文物，一个一个地找到答案。

楼台文化

佛教传入后到南北朝时盛行，当时建造了大量佛寺，佛殿庄严巍峨，成为当时建筑的一个亮点。这里要特别说一说唐代的四大名楼：黄鹤楼（湖北）、岳阳楼（湖南）、鹳雀楼（山西）和滕王阁（江西），它们中三个都是在唐代初期建造的，而黄鹤楼造得更早，它们雄伟大气，飞檐画栋，结构装潢精细，代表了盛唐时期的建筑艺术水平。四大名楼经过历代修缮，精心保护，今天仍以原来的风姿，在原地卓然屹立（其中滕王阁于20世纪80年代在原地按原来面貌重建，鹳雀楼被黄河之水冲坍湮没已久，近年来也已按原貌修复），所以它们今天已成为中国历史建筑的骄傲和瑰宝，其中的两个楼，并不因为是近代重建而影响它们的辉煌。楼台文化的主要意义还不在于楼台本身，而是在于：第一，它反映了中国早期旅游文化的趋势，从唐代开始，全国许多地方，都在名山大川的风景最秀丽处建造楼台，供旅游者观光，大景点造大楼台，小景点造小楼台，遍地开花。除了四大楼台外，还有不少楼台也是非常有名的，像河北的幽州台、江苏的凤凰台等。旅游者到了一个旅游胜地，一登上楼，远近的山水风光尽收眼底，省得他们走许多路，也许还看不到最好的风景。从这里可以看到，中国人很早就是一个爱好旅游的民族，而且，当地政府也乐于做此类公益事业。第二，也是楼台文化更重要的，历代许多著名的文学家和诗人墨客，写下了许多关于楼台的诗、词、文、赋，脍炙人口，像李白、杜甫、韩愈、白居易、崔颢的咏岳阳楼和黄鹤楼的诗，王之涣的诗句"欲穷千里目，更上一层楼"，王勃的名句"落霞与孤鹜齐飞，秋水共长天一色"，它们都是中国文学宝库中的珍珠，给各个楼台铸上一个个不朽的光环，这就是说，诗文的光环比楼台本身更加巍峨高大，它们将同山河永存。

皇宫和民间建筑

　　建筑文化总的包括两种类型：宫廷建筑和民间建筑，宫廷建筑包括皇宫、庙堂、庙宇及高级府第等，往往代表一个社会的建筑艺术和技术水平。而民间建筑与此有联系，又有不同。先来说宫廷建筑，汉代就建造了巍峨突兀的未央宫、建章宫等，唐代又建造了大明

故宫太和殿

宫。这些宫殿，因历史久远，早已变成尘土和历史记载，现今存在的最早最大的皇宫——北京故宫，是明代的建筑。关于故宫，人们如果没有亲自到过，也在电影电视里看过，它的特点是大（气派大）、巍（巍峨雄壮）、威（威武森严）、丽（富丽堂皇）。宫殿的屋顶最有特色，大屋顶，四面尖角高高翘起，下面木柱、斗拱、屋檐，构成承重系统，又显得庄重大方美观。宫殿有一条中心轴线，隔一段，造一座宫殿，隔一段，再造一座宫殿，两边是对称的厢房。中国宫殿为什么有这样的风格？它的背后又有什么文化？这是因为，中国皇帝是所谓真龙天子，是龙的化身，是天帝的儿子，所以，天子的这种天威首先要在宫殿建筑上表现出来，房子住得是不是舒服倒是次要的。例如，宫殿是皇帝召集大臣们商议国家大事的地方，建筑的特点，就是体现皇帝的绝对权威，皇帝威严地高高地坐在龙榻上，下面的空地供大臣们下跪磕头，三呼万岁。

关于民间建筑，现在由于注意了文物保护，明末清初的建筑和建筑群还是比较多的。中国这么大，南方和北方，尤其是少数民族的地区，人们建造的住宅可以说是千差万别的。不过，无论差别怎么大，民间建筑还是有它的共同点的：第一，是把祭天地祭祖宗放在突出地位，表现在房屋的布局，朝南正中，必定是一个大厅，这里最重要的家具是一张供桌。正面墙上，平时挂着书画对联，也作为会见宾客亲友的地方，到了节日或各种纪念日，墙上就挂上菩萨、神仙画像，或祖先画像，摆上祭品，焚香烧烛，顶礼膜拜，大厅旁边的边房或厢房才是生活用房。第二，中国的传统是大家庭，一般是三代同堂，老一代夫妻和几个儿子媳妇及一群孙子孙女居住一起，女儿嫁出去住在男家就不用管了，俗话说"嫁出的女儿泼出的水"。所以，民宅多用四合院形式，住房分配表现长幼有序原则，吃饭在一张大桌面一起吃。媳妇进门以后，要孝顺公婆，听从丈夫，尽力干家务事，一般是没有地位和发言权的，所以那时大家庭的婆媳关系，媳妇是受欺压的一方，不能反抗。再来讲现在中国的家庭结构，民间约定俗成的规则是，一对青年要结婚，就组建一个小家庭，在农村，都是由男方父母提供婚房，所以，许多农民辛劳一辈子，唯一的目的，就是攒钱造几间房子给儿子结婚。在城镇，一般也由男方父母提供住房和家具，女方父母则提供床上用品。中国民间建筑第三个共同点是，房屋总的造型风格崇尚简朴，一般社会地位和经济条件中等的家庭造房子，除了注重外形美观、屋顶式样多变外，一般都是青瓦白墙，地上铺青砖或青石板，因此，无论是单独一户人家，还是一个建筑群落，看上去都简朴大方，表现了中国民居的鲜明风格。

苏州园林

园林是中国特有的建筑，是中国建筑文化的另一个亮点，园林和一般大户人家住宅后面的后花园完全不一样，它是房屋和花园融为一体的建筑形式，屋在园中，园中有屋。园林有皇家园林和民间园林两大类，皇家园林的代表是北京的颐和园和承德的避暑山庄，民间园林南方北方都有，尤其在长江以南，散布着一批很精致有价值的园林，各有特点，其中以苏州的几个园林最为著名，由于篇幅关系，这里重点来说一说苏州园林。苏州园林都是清代的建筑，过去有些读书人一生做官，攒了钱，退休后或回到家乡，或选一个风景较佳的地方定居，他们在当地造园林置田产，以安享晚年。苏州地处江南水网地带，物产富饶，经济发达，交通便捷，风景也很秀美，因此成了许多人落户的首选。在设计园林的时候，房屋建筑和周围景色要统筹规划，一般先挖一个水池，挖起的泥土刚好堆起一个小山坡，山坡上建一个小亭子，同时造成人造瀑

苏州拙政园

165

园林中的曲折走廊

布或泉水。水池周边的假山石是很重要的，假山石有两种，一种是小块的，另有一种大块的，风姿秀丽，独立成风景，有特殊的装饰性。园林中的一栋主体房屋一般都被池水环抱，有栏杆靠水，其他的楼台亭阁，或用树木竹林点缀，或有长廊相接，有分有合，有密有疏，曲尽其妙。还有，园林的一个共同点是，整个占地面积虽然不大，但要造出深不可测的效果，前面景色不能一眼看穿，强调一个"藏"字，有时曲径通幽，有时竹林挡道，转一个弯峰回路转，又出现一个新天地。关于园林的名字，因为园林的主人都是读书做官的人士，所起的名字自然是力求高雅，具有诗情画意的境界，例如，苏州一个最大的园林"拙政园"，主人取这个名字的意思，是说他是一个不善于做官，不愿意和政治圈子同流合污的人，这分明是自己在标榜清高。还有一个园林的名字叫"网师园"，意思是要以结网的渔翁为师，渔翁和渔夫是文人眼中最清高的人，这同样是说自己是一个不计名利，具有高尚情操的人。除了园林的名字，包括园里所有楼台亭阁的名字，都全是什么梅兰竹菊啊，风花雪月啊，超尘脱俗，非常有诗意。这些园林的主人，明明做官赚得金满堂银满堂，有这么多钱造园林，还要有更多的钱供生活开支，吃山珍海味，周围婢仆成群，但表现出来的却是看不起金钱，一说到金钱就等于低级趣味了，整天做些琴棋书画等风雅的事情，这就是中国文人的一种特有的文化。

Chapter 17
Architecture And Garden

E'fang Palace and Qinshihuang Mausoleum

Chinese architecture culture took its shape in the Spring & Autumn Period (770—476 BC) when the emperors of tens of sub-states built their capital cities. The houses began to show the refined layout and structure made of wood and bricks. The Emperor Qinshihuang (the first king of Qin Dynasty), after unified the country and came to possession of whole nation's wealth, launched a campaign to build three big historically-wondered projects: E' fang Palace, Sihuang Mausoleum and the Great Wall. He drove million of war prisoners (whom the tyrant treated resembling animals and cattle) to do the corvee labor. E'fang Palace was a cluster of buildings extending for 15 li (7.5 km) situated at west of Xi'an City, Shaanxi Province, that showed by the time the top level of architecture art and construction technology. Du Mu, a famous poet in Tang Dynasty, wrote a renowned rhymed prose *E'fang Palace Verse* describing majestic spectacle of

Emperor's mausoleum

the palace and criticizing the tyrant's extreme rapacity and squander. Qinshihuang Mausoleum was publicly regarded to be the miracle of the miracles in the world. Some forty years ago, a peasant picked up occasionally some broken pottery pieces that led the discovery of an underground terra-cotta warriors and horses array stirred up people all over the world. But archaeologists declared the array was only a small corner of iceberg of Qinshihuang Mausoleum. Archaeologists have ascertained the true appearance of the tomb by availing advanced scientific means, but they inclined to refuse to cut open the tomb and unearth relics right now, because the relics couldn't protected well by present level of science and technology. Ancient people took constructing their tombs seriously and brought a lot of treasuries with them into the tombs, as they believed they would go to the nether world that something resembled the lifetime society. There were thousands of thousands tombs of emperors and other aristocrats scattered in China's broad territory, and the tomb construction also surely became a part of Chinese architectural art and technology.

Pavilion Culture

There were four super-pavilions in China: Huanghe (literally meaning yellow crane) Pavilion in Hubei Province, Yueyang (south of Mount Yue) Pavilion in Hunan

Province, Guanque (stork) Pavilion in Shanxi Province, and Tengwang (Prince Teng) Pavilion in Jiangxi Province. Among the four super pavilions, three were built in early Tang Dynasty some 1,400 years ago, and Huanghe Pavilion was believed to show up even earlier. In Tang and Song dynasties, many local governments constructed pavilions in scenic places making convenient for people to sightsee beautiful landscapes. Now the four super-pavilions were all preserved well and standing loftily at their original scenic spots due to the careful protection and renovation through generation by generation.(Tengwang and Guanque were rebuilt in recent tens of years) The four super-pavilions were delicately designed and meticulously constructed, and became

Chinese traditional architecture

the symbol of glorious architectural level of prosperous Tang. Besides, the pavilion culture also conveyed China's another two cultural tendencies: One was that Chinese people were the tour-conscious people for a long history, and the other one was there were famous poets and men of letters through many dynasties composed a lot of classical and brilliant poems and rhymed prose when they ascended the pavilions. The literature masterpieces actually made the pavilions much-anticipated, and people regarded them as the eternal aureoles that would make the pavilions long-lived along with beautiful mountains, lakes and rivers.

Imperial Palace And Folk Residence

Imperial palace always reflected the highest level of architectural technology of the time. Historians believed there had been majestic and splendid palaces built in Han and Tang dynasties in Xi'an City, Shaanxi Province. It was said the Da Ming Palace of Tang Dynasty was of three times the size of present Forbidden City in Beijing. The layout of the palace reflected a special tradition of Chinese cultural, the dragon tradition. In the past, emperor was regarded as "the son of Heaven" or "dragon's incarnation", so the architecture style of palace must show off dragon's lofty and absolute power, especially the big and gleaming roof with its four corners highly raised toward the sky. Inside the palace, the "dragon's seat" placed high on the stage was awe-inspiring, and the broad space below the stage only provided officials to line up and play kowtow. As for the styles of folk residence, though there were some differences among different regions or owners of different economical conditions, there was one thing all the same that there was a main hall south-facing and occupied the center of the residence. The hall was a place available worshiping the Heaven and family's forbears. In addition, Chinese traditional big families were usually "three generations under a roof", that made the layout of the traditional folk residence to be a style of "siheyuan", meaning "compound with houses around a square courtyard". In China there was an old tradition still prevailed both in city and countryside that when a young couple was going to marry, the boy's parents were required to prepare a set of

Landscape of Suzhou garden

wedding residence. As a result, most of the parents, especially the peasants have to endure their life-long painstaking labor, for the sake of constructing some wedding houses for their sons.

Suzhou Garden

Suzhou is a modern commercial city one-hour drive west of Shanghai. Suzhou also boasts of its rich history of thousands of years and famous for its several folk gardens original and ingenious in design and flavor. The garden was not the kind popularly seen in the rear of houses only with lawns and trees. It was a compound blended with houses and scenery. There were imperial gardens featuring occupied a broad land including mountains and water in north China, such as the Summer Palaces in Beijing and Chende. And Suzhou private garden featuring occupied only a limited land to form a small and exquisite scene. The garden designer at first dig a pool, piled up the earth into a hill, and built a main residence flanked the water. The whole garden was strategically placed and decorated with pavilions, corridors, curiously-shaped rocks, trees and flowers, as well as bamboo forests. Suzhou gardens were mostly built in Qing Dynasty. Some officials, who collected a plenty of wealth through their tens of years of office time, would plan to enjoy their happy remaining years after retirement by building up exquisite residence and purchasing arable lands. They usually gave their gardens a noble and refined name. For instance, the biggest one of the Suzhou gardens was named "Zhuo Zheng Garden", literally meaning "aloof from politics", i.e., the garden owner described himself as an honest and upright official. Another garden was named "Wang Shi Garden" meaning "learn from fisherman", describing the owner was unwilling to seek fame and wealth. But, where their wealth came from? People could see, in old time Confucius disciples' behavior always unmatched their words.

中医的天人合一论和辨证施治

中国传统的医学和医药，相比于西医西药，有完全不同的理论体系和治疗方法。不像西医建立在严格的科学实验的基础上，中医许多方面缺乏科学论证和数据，所以直到现在，还被崇尚科学的人看作是"巫术"，甚至在最近，国内还有这么一些人主张取消中医中药，闹得沸沸扬扬。但是，数千年来，中国人依靠它治病防病，它的效果是不容否定的。事实证明，中医中药在某些方面独树一帜，它是全人类医学文明的一个重要组成部分。

中国最早的一本医学宝典叫《黄帝内经》，但它其实是汉代人写的。这本书提出了中医的许多基本理论，例如一个根本的理论基础叫"天人合一"，意思是，人是天地间一个生物，所以两者是紧密结合在一起的。例如春夏秋冬四季变化，对人体必然产生影响，冬天寒冷，血管变硬，影响血压，夏天出汗多，人体水分减少影响血黏度。春夏人体消耗大，秋冬适宜储存能量等。天人合一的理论又产生出中医两个基本观点，一是阴阳平衡，中国的古代哲学家早就认为，整个世界是阴阳平衡的产物，太阳是阳，月亮是阴，白天是阳，晚上是阴，男人是阳，女人是阴，南边是阳，北边是阴……任何事物都是阴阳相对而存在。

遍尝草药的神农氏

李时珍采药图

在一个人体内，同样也需要阴阳平衡，当阴阳平衡时，身体就健康，如果健康出现问题，往往是平衡被打破的缘故。所以中医看病，首先要分清病人是阴衰还是阳衰的问题。中医的另一个基本观点就是辨证施治，认为人体是一个整体，一个器官有病，会影响其他器官，全身状况会影响局部器官的变化，同时生理会影响心理，心理会影响生理，所以，辨证施治用通俗的话说，就是从全局着眼进行治疗。这就像自然界发大水，主要根源可能在源头的水土流失，所以要治水，不能就事论事，而是要从全局进行综合治理。

中药主要是用草药，也包括一些昆虫和矿石，副作用比较少，但是，治病的关键在于诊断，过去中医诊断疾病的基本方法是望、闻、问、切四个字。望是看病人的脸色和患病部位，闻是听和嗅，问是询问病人的病史和症状，切是切脉，也就是把脉，医生用三个手指按住病人的手腕，检查脉搏跳动情况，脉搏会显示出病人身体大体的趋势，哪个器官有病，甚至妇女怀孕也摸得出，叫做喜脉。中医这套诊断方法完全依靠医生本人的经验，年纪大、经验丰富的中医不但能够正确诊断出一般病症，还能诊断治疗许多疑难杂症。

中国数千年来出现过不少名医和神医，这里不一一介绍，只提两位家喻户晓的名字：一个是三国时期的华佗，是个外科医生，他为蜀国大将关羽的手臂治疗箭伤，刀子刮得骨头吱吱响，关羽一边下棋一边谈笑风生，这是因为华佗用了针灸麻醉手术。后来华佗为魏国君主曹操治头痛病，曹操生了脑瘤，华佗提出来要做头颅开刀，曹操说华佗是敌国派来的奸细，把华佗给杀了；另一个是明代的李时珍，他曾经在皇宫当过太医，阅读过历代医学书籍，发现有很多错误，于是他下决心要编写一本医书。从1552年开始，他遍历湖北、江西、江苏、安徽、河南、河北等地，收集药方，广泛为人治病，参考前人经验，经历二十余年，终于写成一部巨著《本草纲目》。《本草纲目》出版不久就传到日本，又传到朝鲜和越南，17世纪传到欧洲，先后有德文、法文、英文、拉丁文、俄文等翻译本，国际公认这部著作是对世界医学和生物学的一个巨大贡献。

奇妙的经络和针灸

中国人的祖先用针灸治病，据说在新石器时代就有了，那时候人们把石头的一头磨尖，用它刺激身体上的疼痛部位，金属发明后，金属针代替了石针。所谓针灸，针是用针刺，灸是在针的另一头裹上一点药草，用烟熏，以加强刺激作用。针灸是中医治病的重要组成部分，春秋时期，有一个诸侯国的年轻王子，有一天突然昏厥倒地，两三天过去了，周围的人都认为他死了，这时候，恰好有一个医生路过，他询问了情况，仔细看了王子的病情，拿出随身携带的金针，在王子的头顶周围、脸上和身体几个地方刺了一会，不久，王子的手脚开始活动了，后来眼睛睁开了，身体能够坐起来了，最后他居然起死回生。这个医生就是历史上有名的扁鹊。

中医针灸的基本论点是，在人体全身分布着许多经络和经脉，它们是交通干道，输送着人体需要的能量，中医称为气血。在经络和经脉周围，又散布着许多经穴，也叫穴位或穴道。经络和经脉又和人体的各个器官相连，当经络和经脉畅通时，人体的器官就运行正常，当它们某一个部位堵塞不通时，人体的相应一个器官就不能正常工作，就要生病了，这时候，只要找到相关的穴位，插进金针刺激它，激发经络和经脉的自身活力，达到重新畅通，疾病也就消除了。到了唐代，医学家已经确定全身的经络和经脉，以及654个经穴，并且画成一幅大型彩色针灸挂图。宋代一个医官制作了一个铜人模型，每个穴孔打一个小洞，专门用来教育学生，考试的时候，用蜡把小洞封死，铜人灌满水，穿上衣服，学生拿着针，如果刺中穴位，就会有水流出来。针灸治病还

针灸铜人

有一个独一无二的优点，就是它没有副作用，中草药还有一点副作用，而它一点也没有，即便入针的穴道错了，对身体也没有任何伤害。不过，中医的针灸治病一直遭到西医的质疑和否定，这是因为，经过科学家对人体的解剖，使用了先进的科学仪器，发现人体内根本没有什么经络和经脉痕迹，穴位更不必说了。直到最近数十年，随着全世界一股回归自然的思想潮流的兴起，由于中医采用草药，对人体副作用比较小，逐渐引起人们的关注，同样，针灸也因为它在治病的实践中，表现出不容置疑的效果，而且对某些病症的治疗有奇效，西医束手无策的，针灸医生能够做到针到病除，因此，它也开始被人们广泛承认。现在已经有不少世界各国的医生和年轻的医学院学生，到中国来学习古老的针灸技艺，在全世界许多地方，已经开办了许多针灸治疗所，针灸治病已经受到病人的广泛欢迎。另外，这里顺便提一下，中医还有刮痧和拔火罐的治疗方法，它们的治病原理和针灸完全相同。刮痧是用一块磨平的牛骨，在病痛的位置或穴位上，顺一个方向一下一下地刮，直到皮肤出现紫血块。拔火罐是用一个小玻璃罐，把火伸进罐里烧一烧，很快贴到皮肤上，因为罐里是真空的，皮肤就吸住它，过几分钟皮肤也会出现紫血块，中医认为这种紫血块是人体里的淤血，淤血被清除出来后，身体内的经络和经脉就畅通了。针灸、刮痧和拔火罐，几千年来，在中国一直很流行，不但治病效果好，尤其是治病的费用很低，所以深受一般平民百姓的欢迎。

中医的优越性

前面说过，西医建立在严格的科学基础之上，它自有许多长处，例如采用仪器诊断疾病，准确率高，药物见效迅速，还有一套越来越先进的外科手术系统等，但它也有不足之处，主要是它只针对局部病情，有什么病，治什么病，病情消失就算治好了。西医的优点，一般正是中医的缺点，像诊断手段比较原始（现在中医也配备了西医的各种先进诊断仪器），而中草药的治病效果也比较缓慢。但是，中医有它的优越性，它正好弥补了西医的不足，中医在防治和改善人体器官与慢性病方面有独特的优点，特别是老年人综合性的体弱或器官功能衰退，中医可以采用综合调理的办法，来提高人体机能恢复，或提高防病抗病能力。也有人说，中医只能防病，不能治病，这说法也有失公允。中医不但能治一般的病，也能治细菌和病毒感染性疾病，像老大难的艾滋病和来势汹汹的SARS，西医没有良策对付，而中医运用传统的治疗方法，其疗效也远远胜过西医。值得注意的是，近年来，社会上出现了一个中医群众化普及化热潮，有一些中医医生写了不少通俗书籍，指导一般老百姓怎样进行自我保健强身，甚至治疗自己一些普通的常见病，成了市场热销书。有些中医医生还在互联网上开出博客，和病人互动，互相探讨，搞得非常热火。这些医生主要是指导老百姓怎样利用辨证施治观点，说明人体自身有很大的自我修复机体和自愈疾病的能力，基本方法就是保持经络和经脉畅通，每天做做捶打和按摩身体某一条经脉和某些穴位，简单易行。这是个新的趋向，许多病人在互联网上自述，许多年来折磨自己的疾病，甚至有一些疑难杂症，都意想不到地消失了。正是这个找不到科学依据的经络和经脉学说，在实践中发挥了奇迹般的作用。

药　膳

药膳是中医中药的一个组成部分，望文生义，它就是把中草药放进食物里，做成能防病治病的菜肴。中草药一般都是用水煎成汤药，喝起来很苦，所谓"良药苦口"，现在把药烧成美味菜肴，这真是一举两得了。中国药膳在两千多年前的医书里

药膳（人参豆腐蒸甲鱼）

就有记载，到唐代宋代，一些医书叙述各种药膳的配料和烹调方法，已经十分完备，近年来，有关部门把传统的药膳书籍进行整理，并且加以推广。中医在长期实践中，发现某些食品对人体某一个器官或部位有定向的滋补作用，像羊肉有益肾脏，动物肝脏能够促进造血功能，甲鱼能够养肝补肾，不少食品还具有整体提高人体机能和免疫力，改善体质，像鸡、鸽子、狗肉等。这些东西本来就是美味食品，再加上适当的中草药，烹调成家常菜肴，既保留了它们原来的色香味，而且具有很好的滋补强身和治病作用。

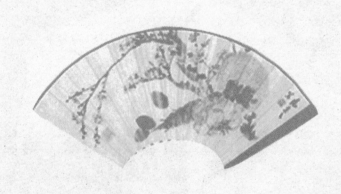

Chapter 18

Chinese Traditional Medicine

Conceptual Basis of Chinese Medicine

The theory and practice of Chinese traditional medicine was differed significantly from that of western medicine. Western medicine put stress on strict scientific experiments, while Chinese medicine was lack of scientific data or testimony, that resulted some people as yet to consider it as a kind of sorcery. But it couldn't be denied that Chinese people had applied the traditional medicine to cure their diseases for thousands of years. The conceptual basis of Chinese medicine derived from a book *Emperor Huangdi's Medicine Classics*, the earliest of the kind in Chinese history. Huangdi was a leader of a primitive community, but the book was written by some unsung experts in Han Dynasty dated back 2,000 years ago. The book brought forward some key viewpoints that became the basis of Chinese medicine theories. The book pointed out: universe and human being blending together, that meant human being was a cell of the universe, so human's health was closely related with every change of the outside world. It also asserted that all apparatuses on human body were connected as a whole, even a man's psychological mood could affect physiology, and vise versa. For instance, a flood could be caused by the soil erosion at the upper reaches of the river. So Chinese doctor won't "treat head when headache, treat foot when foot hurts" toward patient. Chinese doctor traditionally diagnosed a disease by using four steps: watching (patient's appearance), smelling, inquiring (patient's condition) and touching (patient's impulse). Among the four steps, the touching impulse was a key and special diagnosing skill. Doctor put three fingers on patient's wrist and examined the impulse, and he could actually make sense which part of the patient's organ was not functioning well. He could even figure out a "happiness impulse", meaning a woman was pregnant. There were many famous "divine doctors" in Chinese history: One was Hua Tuo in the Three Kingdoms Period (220—280). He could even perform major craniotomy surgery. The other was Li Shizhen in Ming Dynasty (1368—1644). He wrote an authentic medicine book *Bencaigangmu* literally meaning "outlines of herbs", that spread to Japan, Korea and Vietnam, then to Europe shortly after its publishing. The book was widely acclaimed as "a great contribution to medicine science and biology in the world".

Energy And Acupuncture Channels

Chinese ancestors invented acupuncture therapy as early as in Old Stone Era, when people used a stone spear to press the affected point. Afterward, stone spear was replaced by bronze needle. It was said there was a prince of a sub state in the Spring & Autumn Period (770—476 BC) who died of a sudden organ failure. When his family planned to bury him, they were stopped by a stranger who occasionally passed-by. The stranger examined the dead for a while, then took out some needles from his bag, and used the needles to press on some parts of the dead body. It took some half an hour, that the prince gradually regained his consciousness and finally brought back to the life. The stranger was the historically-named doctor Bian Que. Chinese medicine theory believed human's body existed an acupuncture channels net with scattered acupuncture points providing flowing and transporting energy and spiritual strength inside the body. Chinese doctor asserted that a man was usually under a healthy condition when the flowing was smooth, and when a "traffic jam" appeared, some diseases would happen on him. The acupuncture therapy could help dredge the jam by using some needles to excite the acupuncture points. But a lot of western medicine experts have cast much doubt on the acupuncture theory. They, after operating repeated scientific experiments of postmortem, couldn't find any trace of acupuncture channel or point on earth. But on practice, the acupuncture therapy did wonderful job to cure the diseases, especially showing divine affects for what the western medicine felt helpless to cure. As a result, in recent tens of years, Chinese medicine, especially the acupuncture therapy, began to attract more attentions from medicine experts abroad because of its high success rate and low side-effect. Acupuncture therapy won't bring about any side-effect to patients, it even hurt nothing when the needles entered wrong places. In addition to the acupuncture therapy, Chinese traditional medicine also included two similar therapeutic methods: cupping jars and scraping skin, that could also help disperse or discharge the blood jam silted in acupunctural channels.

Advantages of Chinese Medicine

Western medicine has its great advantages as adopting advanced diagnosis machines, efficacious medicine pills, as well as performing series of surgery. The strong points of western medicine were just the weak points of Chinese medicine, but

Chinese medicine could make up the defects of western medicine. Chinese medicine could have special effectiveness for some physical weakness and chronic diseases for old people or delay their aging process by strengthening their constitution. Someone said Chinese traditional medicine was incapable to cure infectious diseases, but in fact, Chinese therapy could also help fight off fatal virus such as AIDS and once showing steamrolling SARS that western medicine faced it helpless. In recent years, a new tendency came to vogue in Chinese community, namely "relying yourself rather than relying doctor". Some doctors wrote books popularizing the knowledge of "do health-care yourself", emphasizing that there was some kind of functions inside human's body available to remedy failing organs, and that people could prevent and cure some common ailments by doing some simple and routine exercises. The most effective way would be striking the acupuncture channels or acupuncture points by one's own fist. The books have won sustained appeal among people both old and young. Some people, afflicted by some serious and complicated disease for a long time, plastered clips on Internet confessing their diseases have disappeared after performing such kind of simple exercise.

Therapeutic Dishes

Chinese ancestors began to cook therapeutic dishes in Han Dynasty, and published therapeutic dishes books in Tang Dynasty. (618—907) The books recorded detailed contents about categories and formulas of different therapeutic dishes. Chinese medicine believed that some food itself contained high nutritive value, such as: mutton was kidney-healthy, soft-shell-tortoise was liver-healthy, and animal's viscera were helpful to hematopoiesis. Chinese herbs medicine was usually ill-tasted, but it would make out a delicious therapeutic dish when cooking the herbs and food stuff together. Now some restaurants brought forth series of therapeutic dishes in a hope to solicit more potential customers, and some publishing houses also republished old copies of

A therapeutic dish

therapeutic dishes books that actually become hot sellers on book stores. People seem more likely to prepare therapeutic dishes by themselves, and the diet therapy could become their favorable treatment helping them stay fit and ward off some diseases.

少林功夫和其他功夫门派

先来简单说一下中国功夫的起源和发展。中国功夫也叫武术，原始社会常发生部落战争，人们就要提高本领，总结技巧，随着社会的发展，战争规模越打越大，也越频繁，人们越来越注重提高武术水平。在这一点上全世界都是一样的，只是中国武术走了一条特殊的路，它是与中国古代哲学和传统文化密切相关的。中国功夫把内功（身体内的精神力量，加上气功）和外功（眼、手、腿的动作）结合起来，最大的特点是讲究招式，包括踢、打、摔、刺，出手凶猛，还要把这些动作连贯起来，形成所谓的套路，并有一个专门名字，像猴拳、醉拳、鸳鸯腿、回马枪，等等。中国功夫除了拳术外，还包括剑、棍、刀、枪等器械武术。在现代武术失去实战意义以后，中国功夫基本上用来表演和强身，当然也有防身作用，这时候人们更注意突出美学，一套拳打下来动作十分潇洒，一招一式造型非常漂亮。

少林功夫今天成了中国武术的象征，河南少林寺名扬海内外，成了一个人们向往的旅游地，对于少林寺和尚的武术传统起源，现在已无法查考，人们认为起初是有些有武艺的人杀了人，逃来当和尚避难，把武艺带进来了。历史上有少林和尚救唐王的故事：唐太宗李世民早年带部

嵩山少林寺

队打天下，有一次兵败，落下一人一骑被敌人追赶，正在千钧一发之际，当中杀出十来个和尚，个个武艺高强，把敌人打退了。唐太宗当了皇帝后，下令嘉奖这些和尚，并且建造了一个规模宏大的少林寺。所以少林功夫的传统，从这时候算起，也已经有一千五六百年的历史了。此后，历代有不少高手把自己的武术奥秘传授给少林和尚，使少林功夫逐渐自成一派，名扬天下。

除了少林外，中国功夫还有一个响亮名字，就是武当派功夫。湖北武当山是座道教名山，武当派功夫也就是道教功夫了。武当教派的创始人是张三丰（前面宗教篇里已提到），据说张三丰的功夫基础来自少林，后来自创一派，另外有个说法是，有一个晚上张三丰梦到天上一个神仙教他武艺，从此他便成了一个武术派别的始祖。张三丰在道教历史上是个辉煌的人物，现在流行的太极拳是他发明的，大概由于这原因，才有他梦见神仙的传说。

不过，中国南北地域广大，千百年来创立各种名目的武术门派的人，实在太多太多，他们创造一门独特的功夫套路，就能够自开一个门派，称雄一时。历史上积累下来的拳法，或棍法枪法，还有许多秘不传人的武术书籍，实在是浩如烟海，略举其中几个，如：象形拳（像猴、鹰、鸭、蛇等形状），迷踪拳（飘忽像影子），罗汉拳（降龙伏虎），醉拳（东歪西倒像醉汉），等等，就足以使局外人眼花缭乱。

太极拳强身

太极拳是一种特殊的健身操，近年来国内练太极拳的人越来越多，尤其是中老年人，同时，它的名声也远播海外。传说宋代（有人说是明初）道士张三丰创造了太极

武当紫禁城

拳，其根据是老子的"以柔克刚"思想，所以，打太极拳和做剧烈的有氧运动不同，一个人打太极拳时动作不快不慢，很柔和，但它的特点是动作连贯，手脚配合，全身协调，特别注意调动身上每一个关节，思想放松，采取深呼吸（深呼

吸有点接近气功，后面要专门谈到）。练太极拳一般要持之以恒，中老年人练太极拳大多数可以收到良好效果，像关节灵活，步履轻盈，心血管功能也会有所改善等。所以，打太极拳是一项宝贵的国粹传统，它对人类的保健却病具有极重要的意义。

今天的太极拳也分了许多流派，都以创始人的姓氏命名，像陈式太极、杨式太极、武式太极等，陈、杨、武都是一个人的姓。除了整套拳法，现在还有了简化太极拳，因为整套太极拳打下来要花一两个小时，所以有人把它简化，保留精华，压缩到二十分钟或半小时，更有利于推广。各种太极拳虽然动作有些区别，它们的原理是一样的，只要认真地练，它们的保健效果也是一样的。

气 功

气功是一种用人的意念指引和控制体内气息的运动，气功的渊源可以追溯到道家，最早叫吐纳术，也叫吐故纳新，就是通过气息运动，把身体内旧的气体排出去，把自然界新的气体吸纳进来，看起来是一种养生保健的方法，但道家理论远没如此简单。道家的许多养生理论起源于黄帝，后来人们称它们为黄老之术。黄帝和老子提出天人合一理念，就是说天和人是相通的，人是宇宙的一分子，每一个人体也就是一个小宇宙。道家认为，人体本来有许多特异功能，这些特异功能随着人的年龄增长而消失，或被封闭起来，而一个人通过修炼气功，打通闭塞通道，可以使特异功能重新回来。既然有特异功能，人们就把它和神仙与长生不死联系起来。世界各地也不时传出一些古怪故事，真假莫辨。在佛教传入中国后，佛教也有一套修炼气功的理论和实践，到后来，佛教气功的影响甚至超过了道教气功。对于特异功能的真假问题，现在科学家之间意见也有分歧，看来，宇宙之大，人类目前的科学，对许多现象尚不能作出解释，还需要作很大探索，对气功和特异功能现象也一样，匆忙加以否定也是不科学的。

气功以功能划分，可以分为硬气功和软气功两部分。硬气功一般融入在武术里，还有用来表演，其实，所有中国功夫都离不开气功。人们现在还常常在电视里看到气功表演，像一个人用嘴咬住一根绳子，拖动一辆大卡车，有的气功师用红缨枪，把锋利的枪尖顶在自己的喉咙或腹部，然后用身体重量压上去。此外，表演者前面放着一叠砖头，至少有五六块，表演者一掌劈下去，砖头齐刷刷地被劈成两半，这说明气功也是有实战用处的。

另外一种软气功，它主要用来保健强身，一般做气功的姿势是，两腿盘膝而坐，眼睛似闭非闭，两只手放在腹前，但是意念如何走，各个门派有各自不同的模式和步骤。现在的软气功除了静坐外，还有站式、自由坐式、躺式，就是说，不论在工作中休息一下，还是躺在床上，随时随地都可以做气功。气功确实有很好的防病祛病功效，但是做气功不能保证一个人不生病，生病了还应该看病吃药。总之，人们如果想自我强身保健，激发自身免疫力，维护调节人体机能，进行气功锻炼，也是一个较好的选择。

中国功夫走向世界

现在中国功夫的名声已经走出中国，走向世界，数十年前，少林寺已经有来自西方的"洋和尚"在那里拜师学艺，现在，到少林寺来学习少林功夫的外国人越来越多。中国这个遥远的东方大国，对许多外国人来讲都很神秘，他们通过中国功夫开始了解一点中国，引起对中国文化的兴趣。说起这个使外国人了解中国功夫的媒介，功夫电影功不可没。

提起中国功夫电影，必须说一说李小龙。李小龙（1940—1973年）原名李振藩，英文名字叫Bruce Lee，出生在美国，在台湾度过少年时期，期间曾师从武术家叶问学习功夫，后来又到美国上大学。他在大学里组织了一支中国功夫队，后来挂牌为"振藩国术馆"，广招学生教授武艺，组织学生到校内外表演和进行友谊比赛。1964年，李小龙在美国参加万国空手道比赛获得冠军，接着，他又在佛罗里达州华人街，一人赤手空拳制服四个持刀歹徒，救下一个华人姑娘，这些消息在报纸上披露后，李小龙的名字和他的功夫开始为美国公众知道，他的国术馆也因此威望陡增。开始，李小龙只在好莱坞参加拍摄一些动作片，20世纪60年代后期到香港主演了《唐山大兄》、《精武门》等功夫电影，立刻在香港、在美国，甚至在全世界引起轰动，美国报刊称他为"功夫王"，德国汉堡大学选他为"最被欧洲人认识的亚洲人"，国际权威武术杂志《黑带》评他为"世界七大武术家之一"，等等。这以后他开始自立门户，同时和美国华纳公司合拍后来影响更大的《猛龙过江》、《死亡游戏》、《龙争虎斗》等影片。但就在他的事业如日中天的时候，他在香港突然死亡，年仅三十二岁。李小龙以三十二年人生、五部影片，成就他不朽的声誉，他是把中国功夫传播到全世界的第一人。

Chapter 19
Chinese Kung Fu And Tai Ji

Shaolin Kung Fu And Other Kung Fu Factions

Shaolin kung fu was an age-old traditional martial art passed down among the monks of Buddhist Shanlin Temple in Henan Province. Shaolin Temple now enjoyed a high reputation both in home and abroad as a sacred place of Chinese kun fu, and meantime became a hot tourist attraction as well. It's hard to say when and how shaolin kung fu took its shape, only some legends recorded in unauthentic books said that the initiators of the kung fu might be some outlaws who fled from crimes and came to the temple lying low, and passed on their kung fu to the monks. There was a popular story about "18 monks rescued Tang prince", describing: Li Shiming, (later became the founder king of Tang Dynasty) was once chased by enemy troops after a defeated battle. At the very critical moment, 18 monks rushed out of nowhere and came to his rescue. They broke up the chasers. After Li acceded to the throne, he issued a citation to the monks and granted to build a spectacular new Shaolin Temple. The event took place some 14 hundred years ago, and people believed the real history of Shaolin would be dated back much earlier. Since then, many powerful kung fu masters in following dynasties came here and passed on their original and exclusive skills to Shaolin monks. Gradually Shaolin kung fu collected and gathered the essence of Chinese traditional martial arts and reached its peak.

Besides Shaolin, there was also another glorious name in Chinese martial arts history "Wudang kung fu". The name Wudang was after the Taoist Wudang Mountain in Hubei Province, and with a highly-prestigious Taoist Zhang Sanfeng in early Ming Dynasty as its initiator dated back 600 years ago. Zhang

Chinese KungFu

learned his basic kung fu skills in Shaolin, and afterward created a faction of his own by his ingenious invention blending Shaolin and Taoist kung fu together. Other legend said Zhang once met a celestial in dream who instructed him the super martial skills, so, Zhang Sanfeng also became the inventor of Tai Ji, the shadow boxing. But, there also appeared numerous kung fu factions over thousands of years. Some martial masters who made some innovations of special skill could create their own factions and made them as the "domineer" for a time. This kind of domineer masters appeared all too often, and they left behind multitude of confidential feats, mysterious books and interesting stories, too many to mention.

Tai Ji

Tai Ji, also the shadow boxing, was known popularly as a special kind of health-care exercise that won more and more appeal among mid-aged and old people. As in that mentioned above, Tai Ji was invented by a Taoist Zhang Sanfeng, so, the boxing was designed based on "soft subdue strong", a theory brought forward by Laozi, the founder ancestor of Taoism in the Spring & Autumn Period (770—476 BC). Tai Ji, differed from modern calisthenics, featured a slow and soft movement. When playing, people would loosen their mind, harmonize their movement of arms and legs and do deep breathing. Most of mid-aged and old people could improve their health if they played Tai Ji regularly and perseveringly. They felt their joints more flexible, their walk steps more vigorous, and their cardiovascular system more healthy. As a matter of fact, Tai Ji was a brilliant treasure of traditional health-care heritage.

Qi Gong

Qi gong, also breathing exercise, was also originated from Taoism tradition. The word "qi" was literally meant "spiritual energy", and the word "gong" meant "arts" At the beginning, qi gong was called "magic arts of spitting and inhaling" by some Taoists, that seemed like a health-care exercise through deep breathing. But playing qi gong was differed from regular breathing. When one doing qi gong, a kind of spiritual energy was moving inside the body guided by his own idea. Shortly afterward, the Buddhist qi gong followed in and even took a more favorable condition than the Taoist. They all believed that qi gong was not only a bodybuilder, but also has much far-reaching significances. They believed that a new-born baby could have some supernatural power, but the power was gradually lost along with the increasing of age. And they also believed "Play qi gong could make human being regain the lost supernatural power". But the public opinions, including high rank scientists' ideas toward the supernatural power were different, some in favor, some against. In China, there were many traditional qi gong factions. Some of them were extremely conceited and looked down upon others, hence they afterward involved in politics.

Qi gong could be classified into two parts: strong qi gong and soft qigong. The strong qi gong was a part of kung fu. People could watch on TV of some qi gong performers splitting bricks with their bare palm, or lying on the edges of knives. While the soft qi gong was a kind of physical exercise people took as a resort to improve their health. Now most people who played qi gong usually aimed at to strengthen their constitution, rather than to regain the supernatural power, and those who played soft qi gong for years or even tens of years, confessed that qi gong have really done a wonderful job for them, helped them improve their health and body fitness.

Chinese Kung Fu Known by Outside World

Now Chinese kung fu has gradually known by the outsiders. Tens of years ago, Shaolin Temple began to see some young blonde monks studying kung fu, and the number of overseas monks kept growing in recent years. China, as an old and mysterious country, had aroused much feeling of curiosity and fantasy from westerners. They wanted to know Chinese culture, and Chinese kung fu came out as a first intermediary and

Bluce Lee

bridge for them.

As a media, kung fu film played an important role spreading Chinese kung fu abroad, and especially a man by name of Bluce Lee had become a kung fu movie star won a household name all over the world. But, the name of Bluce Lee might sound still strange for most of Chinese mainlanders, because Lee made him a hero in 1970s, when china was closed up its door from the outside world. Bluce Lee (1940—1973) was born in the US, and spent his childhood in Taiwan. During the time, he learned kung fu under a famous kung fu master Ye Wen, and then backed to the US to continue his college studies. At first, Lee took part in film making in Hollywood, and in late 1960s, he attended Hong Kong film industry playing leading roles in several blockbusters like *No.1 in Tangshan*, *Jingwumen* (a kung fu faction in early 20th century) that quickly captured millions of hearts all over the world. In early 1970s, he created his own career, continued to make films like *Dragon across River*, *Dead Game* and *Fight between Dragons And Tigers* that all be proven to be big hits. But just at the apex of his career, he was died inscrutably in Hong Kong at the age of 32. Lee was the pioneer introducing Chinese kung fu culture to western world, in 1990, he was selected by public to be the "icons of 20th century" sponsored by the US magazine *Time*. He was the only one Chinese to be included.

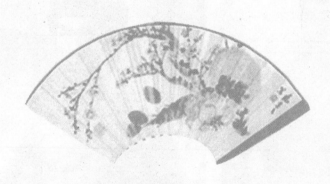

东西方文化交流

郑和下西洋

明代初期，经济复兴，国力强盛，志大有为的明成祖知道海洋之外还有许多国家，加上当时造船和航海技术已经很发达，就决定派遣船队到海外开拓和发展关系。他选定身边太监内侍郑和为统领，因为郑和文武双全，具有将帅之才。和西方早期资产阶级向外扩张殖民不同，明代皇帝给郑和的任务是：宣扬中国文明，建立大国国威，交流财宝，开展贸易。皇帝有一段话，大意这样：边远小国，如果作乱为患，一定要讨伐，如果对中国不造成威胁，我决不讨伐他们。

郑和的船队由两百多艘各种船只组成，最大的指挥船长120米，宽60米，有桅杆9座、风帆12个，船队包括供应船、作战船等，人数达到两万七八千人，都有明确分工。这样庞大的混合舰队，即使是西方一百年以后的船队，它们还是相形见绌。郑和船队一共下西洋七次，第一次出发时间在1405年，只到达文莱、马六甲海峡和斯里兰卡，第五、第六次走得最远，横渡印度洋，到达阿拉伯和非洲东部，最后一次时间是1433年，前后一共历时二十八年。每到一个地方，郑和就向当地国王宣布明王朝对他们的封官，赏赐冠带袍服、金银丝绸和瓷器等物品，建立小国对明王朝的朝贡关系。当

郑和下西洋船只模型

时南洋岛国和东非国家多数还处在穴居火耕时代，男女赤身杂处，用芭蕉叶盛食物，中国人送去衣服、瓷器、钱币等，对提高当地人民的文化和生活习惯起到很大作用，那里的国王也回赠土特产珍品，特别是当时定期来到中国朝贡的国家陆续增加一倍以上，达到三十多个，朝贡的物品五花八门，有珍珠、宝石、玳瑁、珊瑚树、药类、香料，以及狮子、黑熊、猿、鸵鸟等。郑和七下西洋，实行一次大规模的和平外交，以建立一条横跨亚非的友谊桥梁而载入史册。

利玛窦和徐光启

意大利人马可·波罗在元代来中国，回去后写了《马可·波罗游记》，影响很大，欧洲人开始知道在遥远的东方，有一个文化昌盛物产富庶的大国。后来欧洲基督教会曾陆续派传教士来中国传教，但都没有立住脚，主要是基督教的教义，和中国数千年来根深蒂固的儒家理念相悖。到明代末，即郑和下西洋以后两百年，罗马教廷派一些科技精英的传教士来中国，他们中最著名的代表人物就是利玛窦。利玛窦设法把基督教的一些教义和儒家教义融合起来，说他们的上帝就是儒家所说的天，他们的人人平等就是中国的仁和兼爱等等，同时，他利用西方先进的科技知识，首先和中国上层知识分子，尤其是知识型官员建立关系。这期间，他和中国早年科学先驱徐光启的关系，成了中西方科学家合作的第一个光辉范例，他们两人合作翻译的《几何原本》，是一部经典性的著作。徐光启还利用西方先进的数学和天文仪器，重新修订了中国的古老历法，这就是后来沿用数百年的中国农历。在利玛窦和其他几个传教士的努力下，当时中国人信天主教的人数达到十五万人左右。

据说罗马教会对利玛窦等人的传教效果还不太满意，从以后所发生的列强入侵过程来看，基督教是随着洋枪洋炮进入中国，凭借不平等条约强制进行传教的，所以基督教

利玛窦与徐光启

在很长一段时间内，受到中国人的抵制和误解，一直到中国人留学西方的多了，西方文化逐渐为中国人所了解和接受，信基督教也逐渐变成一种时尚，在知识阶层中首先流行开来，基督教在中国的传播，是和西方文化在中国的传播同步进行的。

清代闭关锁国和列强侵华

从清代早年开始，中国实行闭关锁国政策。18世纪末，英国工业革命后迅速崛起，积极寻求海外资源和市场，英国派遣一个代表团，一行七百多人，航行七个月来到中国，目的是想和中国政府谈判通商和建立贸易关系问题。当时清朝乾隆皇帝根本不懂西方的价值观，包括经商、利润、平等、自由等，他认定英国人是来臣服朝拜，要英国人行三跪九叩礼，为这问题双方争执不下，后来同意他们行半跪礼。在会见时，当英国人提出要做生意，乾隆嗤之以鼻，说，我们天朝泱泱大国，物产丰富，什么都不缺，做生意毫无必要，双方意见格格不入，结果英国人空手而归，但英国人利用这次来华机会，摸清了中国的政治经济和军事实力，为50年后发动鸦片战争埋下了伏笔。

1840年鸦片战争爆发，中国国门被英国的炮舰打开，此后半个多世纪，中国沦为列强争相欺侮掠夺的对象。当时英国商人在中国南方倾销鸦片，中国老百姓受害很大，清政府派林则徐去禁烟。林则徐在广东虎门大张旗鼓烧毁鸦片100万公斤，于是英国炮舰炮轰虎门，挑起战争，但林则徐早作了防御准备，英国炮舰就北上攻打上海、南京。清朝军队无法对抗洋枪洋炮，妄自尊大的清政府第一次尝到厉害，慌了手脚，忙和英国人签订屈辱的《南京条约》，内容包括割让香港、开辟通商口岸、赔款，以及允许西方传教士自由传教等。鸦片战争是个信号，使西方列强看到中国懦弱可欺。

1857年发生了英法侵华战争，也叫第二次鸦片战争，直接起因是法国的一名传教士在汕头被老百姓打死。英法联军从天津登陆，一直攻入北京，在北京城肆意抢劫烧杀，把皇宫和圆明园里的珍宝洗劫一空，还把"瑰丽明珠"的圆明园放一把火烧光。清政府再和他们订立屈辱的《天津条约》。在英法联军攻打中国的时候，俄国也趁机在中俄边境出兵，强迫清政府割地六十多万平方公里给俄国。

1894年，即英法战争后三十余年，发生了中日甲午海战，中国北洋水师全军覆没。早在鸦片战争后，朝廷中有一批官员开始动手在国内建立造船厂、兵工厂，向西方国家买武器，还派出几批青年到海外留学，这个学习西方科技的行动叫洋务运动。许多人曾经认为，甲午海战是由于慈禧太后挪用更新海军装备的钱，去建造颐和园，使海军装备落后导致失败，但事实是，当时中国海军装备精良，无论在质量上和数量上都超过日本，主要败因是带兵的各级将领腐败无能，耽于吸毒宿娼，疏于练兵，清朝军队平时欺压百姓，上战场都一触即溃，海军也不例外。海战后，中国的先进军舰都被编入日本海军，在谈判桌上，日本人胃口很大，想独自一口把中国这一大块肥肉吞下去，他们同时陈兵中国沿海，做出攻打北京的架势，以胁迫清政府就范。在这种情况下中日签订了《马关条约》，日本人得到台湾及一系列岛屿领土，得到在东北及许多城市的驻兵权、开矿权、租借权等权益，日本人还提出要中国赔款白银三万万两，这个天文数字也吓坏了清政府，经过讨价还价，最后赔款二万万两。

1900年发生八国联军侵华，起因是当时有一个民间武术团体在北方几个省活动，声称自己身体刀枪不入，慈禧信以为真。这个武术团体就是义和团，他们开始打出"扶清灭洋"的口号，在北京、天津等许多城市主动攻击外国人，于是英、美、俄、日、法、德、意、奥八国组成联军，出动军舰五十艘，军队五万人，义和团总共只有五千人，血肉之躯不堪一击，联军攻入北京，清政府再次屈辱求和，订立《辛丑条约》，各国在中国划分势力范围，当时许多中国人哀叹"国不国矣"（现在还像个国家吗？）。

戊戌变法和孙中山的共和

在中国遭到列强步步进逼的同时，中国人的救民族于危亡的努力也一刻没有停止。前面已经提到洋务运动，到1895年前后，全国已有主张并鼓吹改革的组织、团体三百多个，出版报刊三十多种，《马关条约》的国耻直接促成光绪皇帝变法维新：1898年（岁在戊戌），光绪皇帝颁布诏书，宣布推行君主立宪，发展资本主义，广开言路，开办学校，奖励科学发明等一系列新措施，他重用一批革新人物，像康有为、梁启超、谭嗣同等，罢免了许多守旧官员。而这一切新政触犯了以慈禧太后为总代表的利益集团，慈禧囚禁了光绪皇帝，搜捕革新派人士，康有为、梁启超逃往日本，谭嗣同不愿离开，甘愿以自己的鲜血献给革新事业，戊戌变法只实行一百天便流产了。

孙中山是伟大的中国民主革命的先驱，广东人，甲午战争后，他在日本建立第一个民主革命团体"中国同盟会"，即是中国国民党的前身。他创办《民报》，鼓吹民主革命，第一次提出废除封建王朝，建立共和政体的口号，随后进一步提出民族、民权、民生的三民主义，以及组成一个五权分立（行政、立法、司法、考试、监察）的政府体制的设想。人们看到，中国的封建主义体制是不可能产生民主、自由思想的，生产再发展也不可能产生，有人说，中国封建社会里小生产发展，会产生民主主义，这是不对的，孙中山的民主和自由思想是外来的，因为皇权和民主，两者正好是针锋相对的东西。中国封建主义延续数千年，影响根深蒂固，要中国人接受民主思想也是特别困难的，那时候一般中国人都认为，没有皇帝，那成吗？那还像一个国家吗？1911年，一支受同盟会影响的军队在湖北武昌起义，占领了武汉，十多个省群起响应，宣统皇帝被迫宣布退位，清王朝统治宣告结束，革命派大联合，宣布成立中华民国，选举孙中山为临时大总统，定都南京。不过，孙中山并没有统一全国，这时封建军阀纷纷出来割据，北方军阀窃取了大权，还出现几次军阀复辟当皇帝的事件，革命势力只局限在广东一带，孙中山到最后并没有看到革命的真正胜利。

1919年中国发生五四运动，起因是由于第一次世界大战后，战胜国在法国巴黎举行利益再分配会议，中国作为战胜国，权益受到进一步损害，消息传来，举国激愤，北京学生上街抗议示威，军阀政府进行镇压，事情闹大，全国产业工人罢工，店员罢市，局面失控，军阀政府这才被迫让步，中国参加和会的代表终于拒绝了在和约上签字。

五四运动也是一次文化运动，一批先进的知识分子树起"德先生"（Democracy即民主）和"赛先生"（Science即科学）两面大旗，提出了"打倒孔家店"的口号，提倡新文学，写白话文。"五四"以后，中国文化艺术出现欣欣向荣景象，无论是小说、散文、诗歌、戏剧、音乐、舞蹈等领域，都产生了一批经典性杰作，涌现了一批大师级文学家、艺术家，同时，纯粹的西方文

孙中山像

193

艺样式，像话剧、歌剧、芭蕾、交响乐和电影等，也纷纷来到中国这块土地上落户。

不过，五四运动正是在俄国十月革命后发生，俄国建立了工农兵苏维埃政权，中国一批激进的知识分子转而接受马克思列宁主义，两年后，即1921年，中国共产党成立。

海派文化

什么是海派文化，人们意见恐怕还有分歧，它主要是一种地域概念，指上海加上周边地区有自己特点和个性的一种文化，还包含有海纳百川，容易接受新鲜事物，包括西方文化的意思。中国的文化，南方北方自古以来就有差别，鸦片战争后，上海最早辟为商埠，西方人纷至沓来，万商云集，不久就成为世界文明的前沿。世界上刚有汽车，两个月后上海就有了，世界上刚有电影，几个月后上海就有了，到20世纪三四十年代，上海繁华达到顶点，号称不夜城，有"东方巴黎"的美誉，上海成了东西方文化交流的桥头堡，孕育出自己有明显特点的海派文化。

海派文化最明显表现在建筑上，上海有世界各地各个历史时期的建筑，外滩的一排高楼具有欧洲风采，全市分布着各国风格各异的教堂、别墅和建筑群落等，人们把它们统称为"世界建筑博物馆"，而一般中国人居住的"石库门"房子，中西合璧，式样别致，也成了上海建筑文化的一个亮点。其次就是海派艺术，这个概念比较复杂，20世纪早期，上海有几位杰出的国画大师，极负盛名，只是因为他们居住在上海，所以被称为海派画家。这个时期还有几位京剧大师，他们所演的京剧被称为海派京剧，主要也是地域原因。另外，上海制作的国产电影有时候被叫做海派电影，特别是目前上海的电视节目被叫做海派电视，这就和吸纳海外文化因素有关系了。总的说，上海从辟为商埠近百年来，外国侨民在居民中占了相当大的比例，外国人在上海办的学校也很多，上海人经过长期耳濡目染，受到了比较多的西方人的影响。另外，居民中从海外归来定居的和在海外有亲朋的也比较多，因此，人们从思维方式，到社会风尚和价值观，都染上一层西方文化色彩，有时候人们会评论一个人："这人很海派"，意思大体是说，这个人容易吸收新事物，生活方式比较西方化，等等。

Chapter 20

International Cultural Flow between East And West

Zheng He's Expedition to West Ocean

Early Ming Dynasty saw a revival of economy and military strength of the country. Emperor Chengzu, being informed there were small countries scattered in islands in broad oceans, decided to assign a detachment exploring the region aiming at show off China's power and civilization. He made Zheng He, an eunuch and his chief bodyguard, to be the commander of the expedition fleet. Contrary to the early bourgeoisie expedition troops who targeted to rob wealth and colonize new discovered lands, Chengzu wanted Zheng carrying out a policy of "exhibit China's civilization and create regular relationship with these distant nations", emphasizing "never hurt them unless when they imposed a threat on us".

By the time, China boasted of its advanced technology of ship-building. Zheng He's flagship measured 120 meters in length and 60 meters in width with 12 sails. The fleet consisted of more than 200 ships including combat and logistic ones, and they actually dwarfed the western combined fleets even 100 years later. In 1405, Zheng made his maiden voyage reaching Brunei, Malacca Strait and Srilanka. In 5th and 6th voyages, he went across the Indian Ocean and arrived Arabia and east Africa. When Zheng arrived a new country, he would represent Ming emperor to grant the local chief an official position and a set of official attire, as well as treasures like porcelain, silk and silver coins

The Great Wall

and the sort. During the time, people in these islands still led a primitive life, and the arrival of Chinese fleet could become a contributing factor to promote their life style and civilization. It took 18 years (1405—1433) and seven times for Zheng He to achieve big in his expedition, creating a glorious friendship bridge between China and countries in south Asia and east Africa.

Matteo Ricci And Xu Guangqi

As early as in mid Ming Dynasty, the Vatican had allocated some catholic priests to China to do missionary work, but all failed because the Jesuit doctrine appeared great odds with Chinese tradition. In late Ming, the Church appointed some missionaries of scientific elites to China, Matteo Ricci was the one among them. Ricci, at first, made catholic doctrine compatible with Confucius teaching, by saying that the God for the west was the Heaven for the east, and the universal love for the west was the benevolence for the east. He attached importance to make friends with Chinese high officials who loved science and technology. So the friendship between Matteo Ricci and Xu Guangqi, a great science pioneer in China, became a shining example, and they cooperated to translate a book *Geometry* became a classic handed down to posterity. Xu Guangqi also invented a new calendar system, the Chinese Lunar Calendar, by applying western advanced mathematics and astronomical instruments, and the Lunar Calendar was still used by modern Chinese people. Matteo Ricci and his co-missionaries made increase the number of catholic believers in China over 150,000, but the figure didn't satisfied European Catholic Church. As things happened later, Protestantism resorted mainly to western military to enter China and spread religion by force, and as a result, they would surely be wronged by Chinese as a kind of imperialist cultural aggression. It took a long and complicated process Protestantism was at last known and accepted by Chinese.

Western Powers Invaded China

Qing government carried out a close-up policy toward outside world, just at the time some western industrial powers were eager to launch war to occupy colonies. In early 19th century, some British bizmen devoted to dump large amount of opium in south China that brought about great disaster to Chinese people. In 1840, Qing government appointed a high official Lin Zexu to stop it. Lin, after arrived Guangdong Province, burned out million kg of opium in Humen City. (literally tiger gate) British started up a war but couldn't make their way due to Lin's tight defense, the invaders then went northward and attacked Shanghai and Nanjing. As Qing soldiers' knives and spears couldn't resist invaders' gunfire, the Qing emperor was frustrated and be forced to surrender, and signed the "Nanjing Treaty", the first humiliated treaty of the kind, in which Chinese agreed to ceded Hong Kong, open up commercial port cities, and admit foreign missionaries for their free activities.

The opium war proved China to be weak and easy to bully. In 1857 broke out British-French allying invasion (also called the second opium war). The provoking factor of the war was a French missionary be killed by Chinese in Shantou City, Guangdong Province. After the invaders entered Beijing, they made a big scene of raping, rooting, arson and killing, especially they ransacked treasures in China's imperialist Yuanming Palace unscrupulously, and finally burned out the most spectacular palace which collected most of rare cultural treasures over Chinese thousands of years. During the war, Russians seized a territory of 600,000 square km from China.

In 1894, broke out Sino-Jap sea war, in which Chinese North Navy Force was all annihilated. For a long time, people believed the defeat of Chinese navy was due to lack of renewal of equipments, because Empress Dowager Cixi, a parliament ruler, diverted the budget to build the Summer Palace in Beijing. But the fact turned out not the case. At the time, Chinese navy had finely-equipped ships more advanced and powerful than Japanese navy. The key issue was the officers' corruption and incapability. Qing troops were all skillful to bully people, but always collapsed at first encounter when they went to battlefield, and the navy was surely not excluded. In the conference table, the Japanese showed an appetite to swallow whole China by one mouth. They also disposed military around China's off sea, in a bit to bully China to submit. At last, Japanese obtained Taiwan and other small islands, an indemnity of astronomical figure, as well as the right of stationing military in Chinese lands.

In 1900, took place the invasion of 8-country allying forces. At the beginning, there was a kung fu faction Boxers declared they could thwart bullets with their bare bodies. Empress Dowager Cixi did believe them, so the Boxers began to attack foreigners in cities and countryside. The 8-country troops (British, American, Russian, Japanese, French, German, Italian and Austrian) quickly occupied Beijing, and the Boxers, only 5,000 fighters, all died under gunfire. Western countries then shared their interests they deserved and split Chinese territory to be their colonies.

The 1898 Reform Movement And Sun Yah Sen's Revolution

Along with western powers' invasions, Chinese salvation movements rose up. The humiliation of Sino-Jap sea war became the stimulus of the 1898 Reform Movement. At first, Emperor Guangxu, with the help of his think tankers Kang Youwei, Liang Qichao and Tan Citong, released an order carrying out the political system of constitutional monarchy, developing capitalism. But the policies infringed on the vested interests of privileged conservatives headed by Cixi. Cixi then immediately drove Emperor Guangxu off the throne, and put him under house arrest. The aborted reform only lasted for 100 days, and Guangxu's advisors Kang and Liang were fleeing to Japan, and Tan died a martyr death.

Dr. Sun Yeh Sen was a great forerunner of Chinese democratic revolution. After the Sino-Jap sea war, he created a revolutionary group named "Association" (of which Kuomintang grew out) in Japan, starting a newspaper *People Post* to propagate his political views. He for the first time put forward the idea of creating a democratic government in China, as well as his so-called "Three Peopleism" (strive for people's better life, people's free speech and people's political right). In 1911, a revolutionary troop rose up and seized Wuchang (now Wuhang City, Hubei Province), and the victory made the collapse of Qing Dynasty and founding of the Republic of China. At the national congress of the revolutionary associations Dr. Sun Yeh Sen was selected as China's first provisional president. But, Sun's revolution and new government never brought about national unification in China, the country fell into big chaos due to some powerful war-lords set up their armed separated regimes. The land Sun controlled was only limited in Guangdong Province. In 1925, Sun died of cancer.

In 1919 occurred the May 4th Movement. The reason for the outbreak of the movement was China was humiliated at Paris international conference where the victorious countries of World War One negotiated sharing world profits. At the hearing of the news, students in Beijing took to the streets, gathered at Tiananmen Square and held mass protesting rallies. After the warlord's government arrested a large amount of students, the protesting tides surged all over the country. The political movement soon turned into a cultural movement, some advanced intellectuals brought forward the idea of inviting so-called "Mr. Democracy" and "Mr. Science" to come China's rescue, and others put forward a slogan "Down to Confucius Shop". They also advocated writing "new styled literature", carrying out the vernacular style of writing (people used to write classical Chinese before the May 4th Movement). So the May 4th Movement became a symbol of youth's revolutionary spirits, and gave a far-reaching cultural impact to China's coming young generations.

Shanghai-Style Culture

The meaning of the word "Shanghai-style culture" sounded still controversial among the people. At first, it indicated a kind of culture with special regional characteristics. Secondly, the words Shang and Hai were literally meaning Upper Sea, and there was a saying "Sea has a broad-minded manner to accept the water running down from hundred rivers", so the word "Shanghai-style culture" also indicated the culture was easy to take in new exotic cultures. Shanghai-style culture at first spotlighted the architectural culture. Shanghai for a long time won a reputation as "International Architecture Museum", with a row of European style high buildings in the Bund, also with churches, villas, residential complexes of world's different styles of architectures scattering around the city. And "Shikumen", a kind of common people residences meaning "stone gate" blending east and west

An indoor view of Chinese residence

styles together, became an unique style of architecture in Shanghai. As for Shanghai style arts, it was a little bit more complicated to describe. In early 20th century, there were some icons of painters and Beijing Opera players who were all given a name of "Shanghai-style artists". It was merely because they were staying in Shanghai. But people also called the films produced by Shanghai Film Studio and the TV programs aired on Shanghai TV Station as "Shanghai-style film" or "Shanghai-style TV", it could actually contain another meanings. In recent hundred years, Shanghai has been an important international port city and displayed western-style prosperity. People called Shanghai as "Eastern Paris" or "A heaven of international risks-endeavors". It was said, Shanghai was among a few cities in the world appearing earliest car, telephone and moving pictures (films) . More, there were a large amount of expatriates resided in Shanghai, and at the same time, a large amount of Shanghai families having their relatives staying abroad. As a result, Shanghai became a bridgehead of international cultural exchanges, and Shanghai people have become more westernized due to accepting more western cultures. Sometimes, people pointed a person, saying "This is a Shanghai-style man", that meant the man was more westernized in thinking style and behavior.

图书在版编目(CIP)数据

中国人的文化 / 周济著. —上海：上海文化出版社，
2009
ISBN　978-7-80740-458-3

Ⅰ.中… Ⅱ.周… Ⅲ.传统文化-中国 Ⅳ.G12.

中国版本图书馆 CIP 数据核字（2009）第152785号

出版人
陈鸣华
责任编辑
吴志刚
装帧设计
许　菲

书名
中国人的文化
出版、发行

上海文化出版社

地址：上海市绍兴路 74 号
电子信箱：cslcm@ publicl. sta. net. cn
网址：www.shwenyi.com
邮政编码：200020
印刷
上海市印刷十厂有限公司
开本
787×1092　1/　18
印张
12
字数
230千字
版次
2009年9月第1版　2009年9月第1次印刷
国际书号
ISBN 978 - 7 - 80740 -458 -3/G・491
定价
28.00元

敬告　如本书有质量问题请联系印刷厂质量科
T: 021 - 65410805